THE ART OF

MARVEL STUDIOS

CAPTAIN AMERICA
THE FIRST AVENGER

Written by **MATTHEW K. MANNING**

Book design by **MIKE ZAGARI**

Foreword by **RICK HEINRICHS**

Dustjacket art by **RYAN MEINERDING**

Captain America created by **JOE SIMON & JACK KIRBY**

TITAN BOOKS

FOR MARVEL PUBLISHING
JEFF YOUNGQUIST, Editor
SARAH SINGER, Editor, Special Projects
JEREMY WEST, Manager, Licensed Publishing
SVEN LARSEN, VP, Licensed Publishing
DAVID GABRIEL, SVP Print, Sales & Marketing
C.B. CEBULSKI, Editor in Chief

FOR MARVEL STUDIOS 2011
KEVIN FEIGE, President
LOUIS D'ESPOSITO, Co-President
STEPHEN BROUSSARD, Senior Vice President,
  Production & Development
MICHAEL ROSS, Senior Vice President,
  Business & Legal Affairs
ELIZABETH LYNCH, Senior Vice President,
  Business & Legal Affairs
RYAN POTTER, Executive Counsel, Business &
  Legal Affairs
ERIKA DENTON, Clearances Manager
WILL CORONA PILGRIM, Creative Manager,
  Research & Development
RANDY McGOWAN, Director, Digital Assset
  Management
ALEX SCHARF, Digital Asset Coordinator
ALEXIS AUDITORE, Physical Assets Coordinator

MARVEL STUDIOS: THE INFINITY SAGA -
THE ART OF CAPTAIN AMERICA

ISBN: 9781803365534
E-BOOK ISBN: 9781803365855

First edition: November 2023

10 9 8 7 6 5 4 3 2 1

Published by Titan Books
A division of Titan Publishing Group Ltd
144 Southwark St, London SE1 0UP

www.titanbooks.com

Did you enjoy this book? We love to hear from our readers. Please e-mail us at: readerfeedback@titanemail.com or write to Reader Feedback at the above address.

To receive advance information, news, competitions, and exclusive offers online, please sign up for the Titan newsletter on our website: www.titanbooks.com

A CIP catalogue record for this title is available from the British Library.

Printed in China

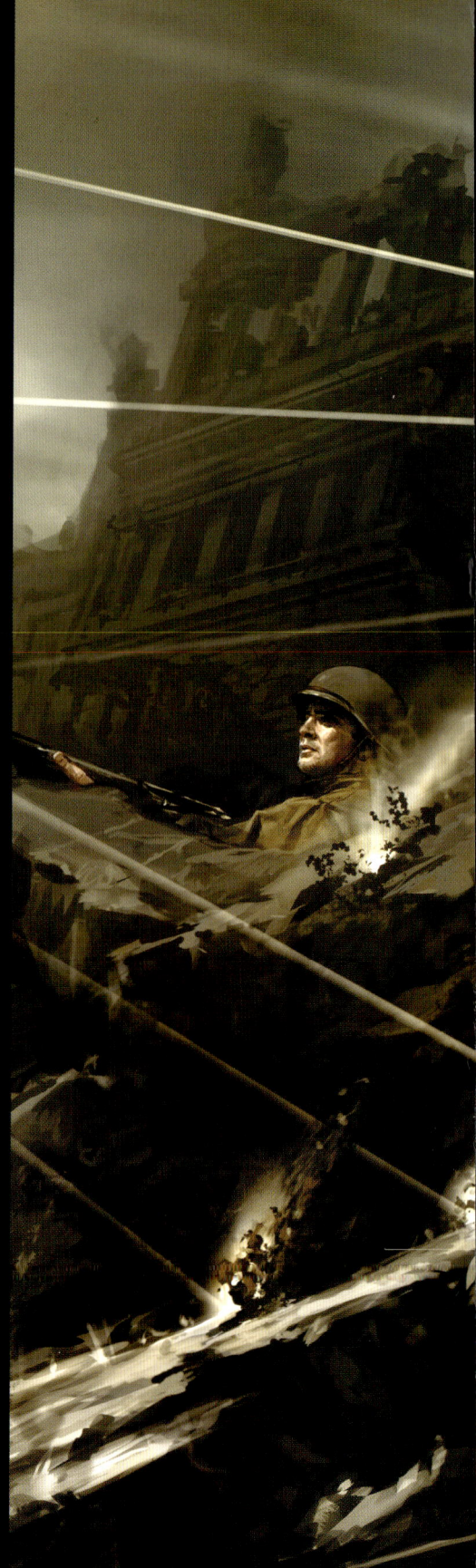

CONTENTS

From left to right: Rick Heinrichs, Joe Johnston and Daniel Simon discuss Hydra vehicle designs in the Marvel Studios Pre-Production offices.

FOREWORD

It was with slight trepidation that I agreed to design Captain America for Joe Johnston and Marvel Studios. I'd worked with Joe before and enjoyed the collaboration with an imaginative, experienced director and superb artist who somehow knew how to make a tough job fun. Marvel Studios had a reputation for caring about the look of the films they made with their well-loved characters, so I was in good hands there. My problem?

It was that my father, a history professor of no small recognition in his field, happened to specialize in the American involvement in the Second World War and to have fought in it. Hewing this closely in a movie based on a comic book to a period and intense experience that in many ways was still very much alive for him gave me pause. I was acutely aware of the danger of trivializing or misrepresenting factual events for the dubious benefit of selling popcorn.

What kept occurring to me, though, was the image of Cap belting Hitler on a comic-book cover that was on the street even before the United States entered that war. Captain America was part of the history of that period, presented by his creators partly as a tool of persuasion intended to coax the United States off the sidelines of that war and shoulder the burden thrust upon it by unprecedented world events. At a time when Americans were emerging from the Depression to dream of a better future, they were presented with the more likely alternative of a bleak, totalitarian, soul-crushing world in which the bully gets away with stomping on the little guy. I read moral indignation behind the creation of the character, and America was founded on outrage against tyranny. While "wrapping oneself in the flag" has come to mean conservatism disguised as patriotism, I think that during this dire time of stark moral imperatives, Captain America's look was an appropriate call for national resolve and action. I decided in the end that my father of anyone would understand the value of using fictional narrative based on fact to examine the cause and effect of an historical event — that is, imaginatively nudging the "story" part of history to reveal truth.

There is an aspect of filmmaking that often reminds me of a military campaign (though not the actual letting of blood — yet!). You have to rally the troops and muster supplies, determine your objective and strategize its accomplishment, allocate your resources, navigate logistical quagmires, and mobilize to fight the battles and ultimately win the war. The First Avenger was no exception to this metaphor. I started designing the film in Los Angeles with my frequent collaborator and Supervising Art Director John Dexter and a fantastic L.A.-based art department. After a worldwide scout for locations, we settled on the United Kingdom — requiring a move to London and a new art department, where the exceptionally capable Chris Lowe joined John in supervising it. Many of the challenges seemed insurmountable — but our resourceful Gen. Johnston always seemed to have another, better idea. We did finally win our battles, and this book supplies evidence of the effort of the talented individuals who created the work that gives form, color and texture to the film.

Rick Heinrichs
2011

THE AMERICAN DREAM

It was 1940, and America was a nation divided. While what would become known as the Second World War raged overseas, the United States stood on the sidelines, its people debating the merits of joining a battle so far removed from their homeland. But in the heart of New York City, comic-book publisher Martin Goodman had no such reservations. Perhaps it was his Jewish heritage that caused him to take offense to Adolf Hitler's twisted Nazi agenda, or simply his need to comment on an unjust situation. Whatever his inspiration, Goodman couldn't just sit by quietly while his country did nothing.

So Martin Goodman declared war.

A full year before the devastating attack on Pearl Harbor that roused the United States into action, Goodman sent one of his most prized troops into battle: Namor, the rebellious Sub-Mariner. Fighting Nazis on the high-profile cover to *Marvel Mystery Comics #4*, the Sub-Mariner blatantly displayed Timely Comics' stance to the country's youth. And that was just the first shot fired.

Cover to *Captain America Comics #1* (1941) by Joe Simon and Jack Kirby, repainted by Kai Spannuth for *Captain America Comics #1: 70th Anniversary Edition* (2011).

Enter writer/layout artist Joe Simon and artist Jack Kirby.

Said Simon, "And comics you had to build your business. If you had a character that was not successful, and you had to go home and figure out another character that would be successful. Otherwise, you're out of work. So we were always trying to come up with something new. Otherwise, we would just sit in our little hotels or roommate houses and wait for a call that never came."

Simon and Kirby took their youthful enthusiasm and began brainstorming a new idea. Said Simon, "At the beginning, Batman was doing very well. Basically, on the use of his villains. The Joker, you know…and then Superman had Lex Luthor…But so I said, 'Maybe… that's the answer. You know, get yourself a good villain.'" And in those days, there was no better villain than the real-life leader of the Nazi party, Adolf Hitler. So Simon and Kirby's true challenge became a matter of finding Hitler's perfect opposite. An opposite they discovered in a new hero named Captain America.

Captain America Comics #1 debuted in March 1941. While other heroes had worn red, white and blue outfits, Goodman, Simon and Kirby permitted no doubt in their political leanings. Captain America wasn't just battling Nazis on the cover of his first issue. He was punching Hitler himself right in the face.

Fulfilling the wishes of many would-be soldiers, Simon and Kirby told the tale of weakling Steve Rogers, whose frail body prevented him from helping the war effort despite his earnest intentions. But with the aid of a top-secret Super-Solider serum, Rogers soon became a perfect human specimen, willing and more than able to lead America into the war against the Nazi menace.

Said Stephen Broussard, co-producer on *Captain America: The First Avenger*, "It was very much viewed as taking a stance, as controversial. The United States was just coming out of the Great Depression, just getting back on its feet. World War I was fresh in everyone's mind. It was very much viewed as Europe's war and Europe's problem — not by all, but by a large segment of the American population. So when you have Captain America punching out Hitler in March 1941, before Pearl Harbor, it's definitely a statement. It was definitely saying, 'We cannot sit by the sidelines anymore.'"

"The original Captain America was a propaganda tool, and it's very clear and it's way over the top. And it would be. It would be called flag waving and jingoism if it were published today for the first time," *Captain America* Director Joe Johnston said.

And it was that direct attempt to influence America's youth that led to Simon and Kirby finding themselves at the center of a heated controversy. "This was the time just before the war, and we were besieged by the American Boon members," Simon said. "They used to have big rallies at Madison Square Garden. They'd have fifty thousand people in the rallies. And they had a lot of sympathizers. They found out where we were, where we lived, and every day… the streets were crowded with the Boon members protesting and spitting on us…They were very aggressive people."

The protests grew so extreme that FBI agents were dispatched to the offices of Timely Comics — the publisher that would one day come to be known as Marvel — to protect the company's comic-book talent.

America soon entered World War II, and the protests dwindled. Captain America was on the front lines with his youthful sidekick, Bucky, fighting Nazi enemies like the horrific Red Skull. With his magazine selling almost in the millions, Captain America had captured the heart of his nation; his adventures even outsold mainstay newsstand publications like *Time Magazine*.

However, World War II finally came to a close. And with the bloody conflict over, America's loudest cheerleader started to lose his voice. Super heroes in general fell out of favor as other genres like horror

AMERICA CALLING

Take your place in Civilian Defense

and crime began to become popular. By 1950, Captain America could scarcely be found in his own magazine; the title had been changed to *Captain America's Weird Tales*. The comic came to a close with issue #75, and Captain America began to fade into obscurity.

By 1954, a change in publishing strategy gave Cap a new lease on life. Taking up arms during the Cold War, the good Captain's adventures began again with issue #76, now boasting the phrase "Captain America, Commie Smasher" on each cover. However, America had changed and seemingly outgrown such

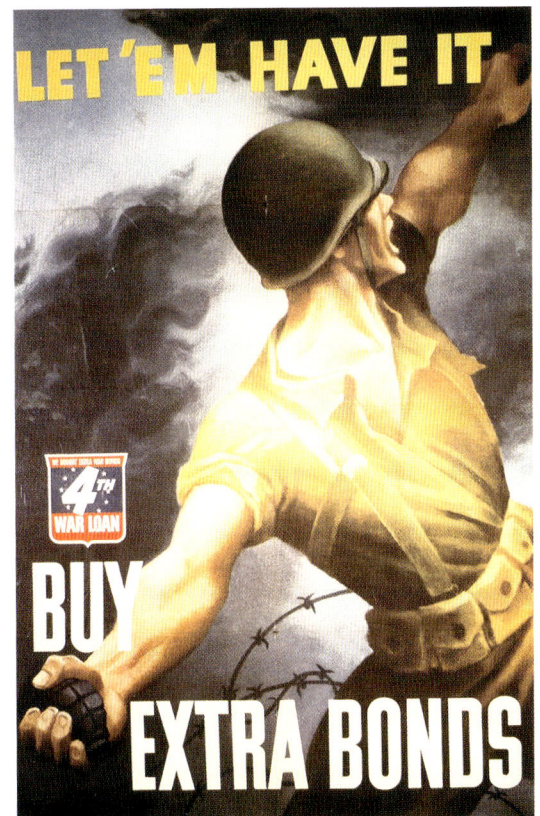

LET 'EM HAVE IT

4TH WAR LOAN

BUY EXTRA BONDS

blatant propaganda. Captain America was soon put on ice once more, until famous comic-book writer/editor Stan Lee took it upon himself to thaw out the old icon.

Ignoring the hero's Cold War adventures, Lee and Cap co-creator Jack Kirby resurrected him into their popular super-hero team book *Avengers* in March 1964 with the conceit that the other Avengers had discovered the World War II icon frozen in an iceberg. Instead of using the hero to coax troops into Vietnam or in support of any other war effort, Lee instead decided to play Cap as a man out of time, wondering what his place was in the brave new world into which he'd been reborn. By questioning his own government and its agenda, Captain America again captured the public sentiment, suddenly becoming just as relevant as he'd been decades earlier.

And it was this reinvention that would keep the hero a Marvel mainstay in the years to come. During the 1970s, he teamed up with African-American hero the Falcon. In the 1980s and 1990s, he found himself at odds with his own government and even abandoned his super-hero identity for a time in favor of a new one: the Captain. In addition to confronting corrupt factions of the government, he faced a more violent version of his crime-fighting persona in the form of the volatile USAgent, outfitted in the uniform Steve Rogers had worn as the Captain.

But it was in September of 2001 that Captain America would truly return to his roots. When terrorists attacked and destroyed the World Trade Center in New York City, the country needed a patriot more than ever. Out of this unified desire for justice came a new *Captain America* series in which Cap took a proactive stance against terrorism. The intent of Marvel and writer John Ney Rieber was as obvious as the covers by artist John Cassaday bearing phrases like "Fight Terror" and "Are You Doing Your Part?"

Captain America was again a voice of his nation, and writer Ed Brubaker soon would capture that constantly shifting dialogue in his critically acclaimed 2004 relaunch of the title. In a country

GUADALCANAL America's World War II ground offensive began Aug 7, 1942, when the 1st Marine Division, Reinforced, landed at Guadalcanal. Through rivers, swamps, and steaming jungle the rugged, resolute Marines fought on until this first great stepping stone to Japan was won.

ENLIST NOW
U.S. MARINE CORPS

ABOVE: Cover to *Captain America Comics #13* (1942) by Joe Simon and Jack Kirby.

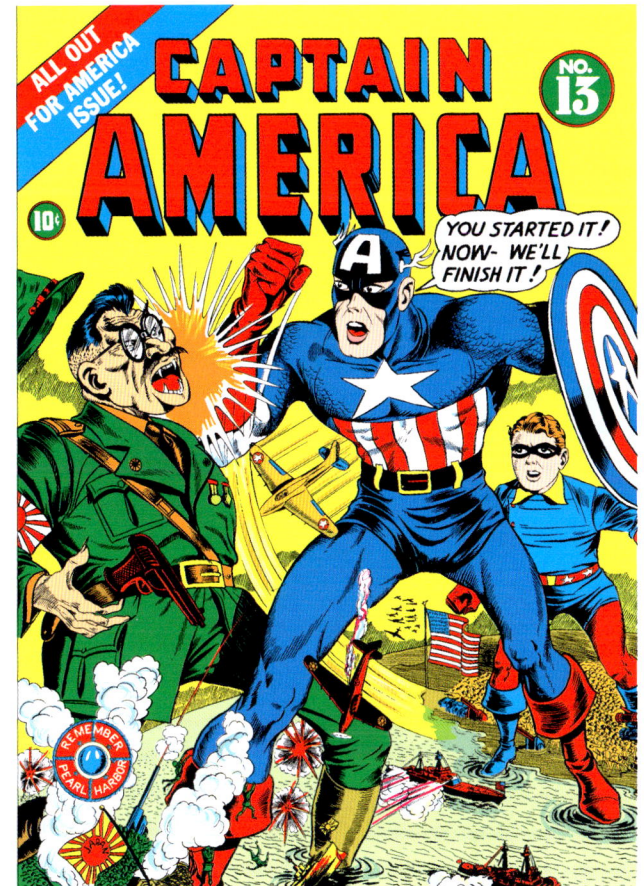

again divided by political leanings, Captain America fell victim to circumstance — shot and seemingly killed in a plot set in motion by the Red Skull. His successor was none other than his former sidekick — Bucky, returned from his own apparent death — and the iconic uniform of Captain America was altered to reflect the world he now inhabited, most prominently with the addition of a sidearm.

LEFT: Cover to *Captain America Comics #2* (1941) by Joe Simon and Jack Kirby.

ABOVE: *Captain America Comics #7* (1941), page 1, by Joe Simon and Jack Kirby.

But while telling a controversial tale of patriotism and the definition of heroism, Brubaker and company soon brought back Steve Rogers. Again at the forefront of America's fighting forces, the noble heroics of the decades-old icon shine brightly despite the darker overtones of today's more violent world. And while his adventures have been captured on film in the past, his story now is being brought to life for the first time in true blockbuster movie fashion.

RIGHT: *Captain America Comics #1* (1941), page 8, by Joe Simon and Jack Kirby.

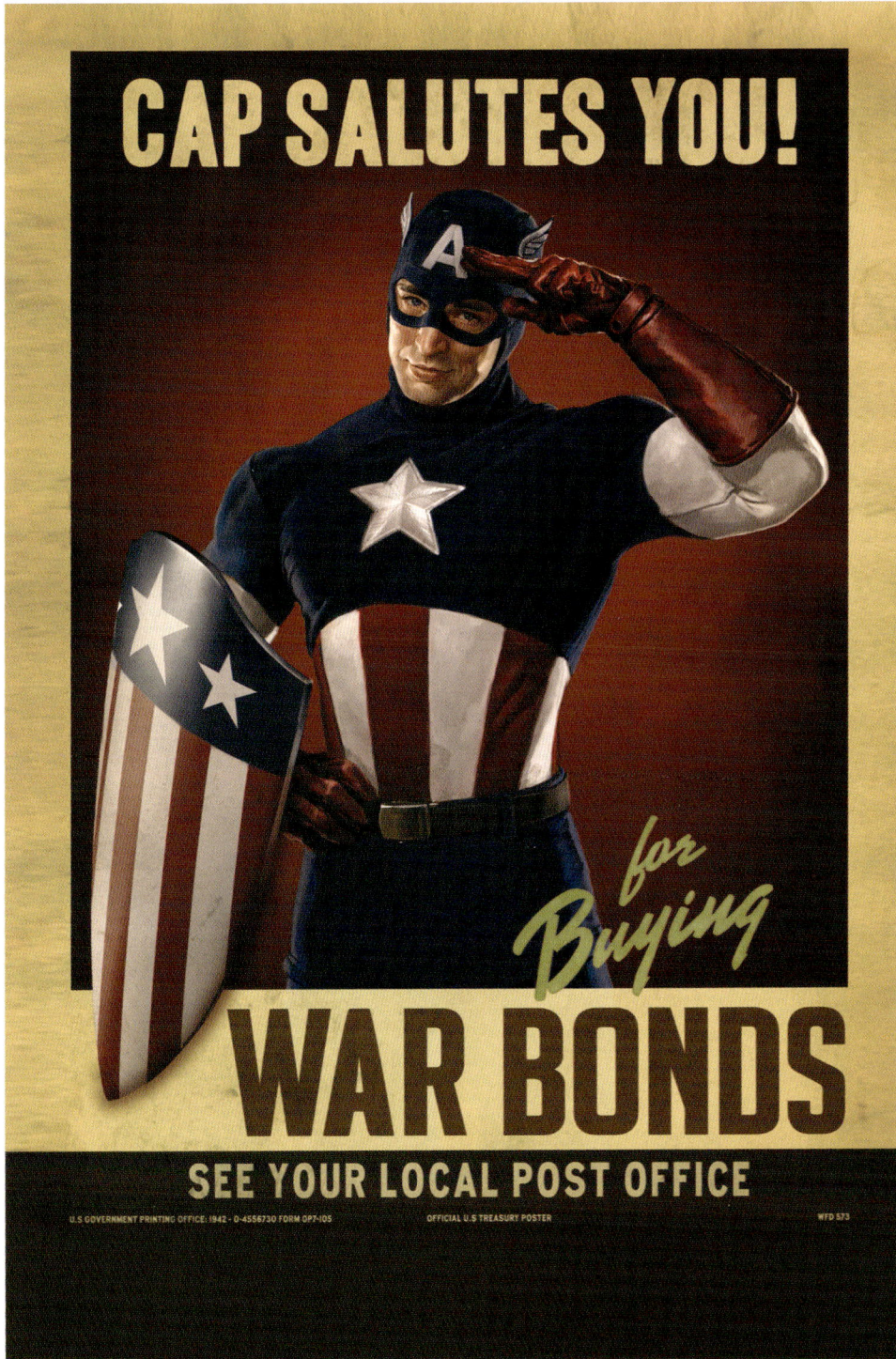

CAP SALUTES YOU!

for Buying

WAR BONDS

SEE YOUR LOCAL POST OFFICE

U.S GOVERNMENT PRINTING OFFICE: 1942 - O-4556730 FORM OP7-105   OFFICIAL U.S TREASURY POSTER   WFD 573

Said Marvel Studios President and Producer Kevin Feige, "What makes Marvel Comics' characters great is that the creators and various writers and artists took chances with the characters over the years, which is why so many Marvel characters change and evolve and grow. And when we make one of the movies, we never want to shy away from that. We want to take the same chances in the course of however many movies we're lucky enough to make in the character's franchise."

He may have evolved, but Cap has never wavered.

"What's fascinating about Steve Rogers as a character and Captain America the character is that he has largely remained unchanged," Co-Producer Stephen Broussard said. "It has become a reflection of the times, a sign of the times, but always through that same perspective. And that is why Steve Rogers as a character will always be here, because he is able to adapt to the times, and he is able to reflect the mood of the country at any given moment."

Added Captain America: The First Avenger Director Joe Johnston, "I think Captain America represents more the spirit of what America is. It's not that he waves the flag and represents the country, it's more the spirit of America and what that means to the rest of the world."

It's 2011, and the United States is a nation divided in its thoughts about war and politics. Once more, Captain America is being introduced to a new generation. It's time again for America's hero to capture the hearts and imagination of his people — just as he did seven long decades ago.

LEFT: WWII War Bonds Poster featuring Captain America, as seen in the film — art by Ryan Meinerding, text by Anita Dhillon.

CHAPTER ONE
THE SENTINEL OF LIBERTY

He's as American as apple pie. Captain America has been a patriotic symbol of the United States for seventy years. He's been a hero, a rebel and a tool for propaganda. He's represented a proud nation through some of its finest and darkest hours. So when Marvel Studios decided to craft Cap's first blockbuster venture, they knew they had to get it right.

"Captain America is one of the most iconic, one of the most famous, well-known characters in the Marvel canon," Producer and Marvel Studios President Kevin Feige said. "There's only one or two characters that are older than that, that have a longer history than Captain America does in the Marvel comics. I would say he's right up there with Spider-Man — his being well-known; his being beloved; his being an iconic piece of comicdom, of Americana — and it's a big challenge to bring him to the screen."

To capture the character's true essence, Marvel Studios opted to start at the most logical point in Captain America's career: the beginning. Since Cap's adventures began in the tumultuous era of World War II, the project quickly became a period piece. And with that decision, the choice of director was obvious.

Said Feige, "I've been a huge fan of Joe Johnston for almost my entire life. *October Sky, The Rocketeer,* his career has been leading up to this — to doing a Marvel period movie that is cutting edge, that is contemporary, that has heart."

Keyframe art by Ryan Meinerding.

CAPTAIN AMERICA : USO

Unlike many super-hero films, *Captain America: The First Avenger* shows a true evolution of its title character. We see Cap undergo the transformation from scrawny youth to a jingoistic figurehead to the hero Marvel Comics fans have loved for generations. And to make Captain America's journey a visual one audiences could identify with, the filmmakers were tasked with developing several different looks for their title character.

The first of Captain America's many uniforms is his USO costume. Chosen to be a test subject for a secret faction of the U.S. government known as the Strategic Science Reserve, Steve Rogers is injected with a serum that transforms his frail body into an idealized form that functions at the peak of human perfection. But instead of fighting on the front lines as he expected, Rogers unwittingly finds himself becoming an exaggerated symbol for his nation, a propaganda tool touring USO camps.

Keyframe art by Ryan Meinerding.

Concept art by Ryan Meinerding.

Production still.

Concept art by Mauro Borelli.

Said Concept Artist Ryan Meinerding, "The USO suit was in a little bit of a strange wiggle room between trying to find how goofy to make it and how honest to Captain America we wanted to make it. I think in the making it ended up going a little bit goofier than I expected it to, but it probably works for the film 'cause he's meant to come to sort of despise what he's going through in that particular stage."

What's more, the conceit of the USO stage show allowed filmmakers to justify Captain America's classic vibrant costume from the comic books. "The USO suit is basically an unadulterated [version] of Captain America's suit," Meinerding said.

USO SHOW GIRLS

A true spectacle reminiscent of vintage Broadway, the USO show even granted Captain America his own background dancers. Said Director Joe Johnston, "They start using Steve as a propaganda tool, put him in a dance number in his Captain America flag suit, and that evolves as he goes AWOL, goes into combat. That's one of the challenges with a film like this. You can't have him really step out of the pages of the comic book onto the screen. You have to interpret the visual palette you've got from the comic book."

Concept art by Darrell Wagner, costume design by Anna B. Sheppard.

24

Production stills.

CAPTAIN AMERICA: POW RESCUE

As the film progresses, Captain America soon becomes frustrated with his role as a mere mascot and embarks on a rescue mission despite the orders of his commanding officer. And since the flashy USO costume isn't a feasible choice of outfit for real-world combat situations, the art department was challenged with designing a new uniform for Captain America — one equal parts patriotic and practical.

To help achieve the look of Cap's POW rescue uniform — as well as his later, finalized costume — Meinerding and fellow Concept Artist Charlie Wen looked to the comic books for a creative spark. Said Meinerding, "I was looking through the Ed Brubaker run; it's such a great story line. That stuff has always been a great inspiration for me."

Concept art by Ryan Meinerding.

"The version in *The Ultimates* is the most modern take that's happened on Cap," Meinerding said. "Looking at what Bryan Hitch did was a big source of inspiration, and I've always loved the Kevin Maguire *Adventures of Captain America* books. We definitely took the idea of Cap's cowl being a helmet with a chinstrap, and incorporating webbing and gear, from *The Ultimates*."

Concept art by Ryan Meinerding.

Production still.

Said Meinerding, "I think one of the things I tried to bring to the design was some sense of realism. So to try to take something that on the page reads as really great — the iconic silhouette that Jack Kirby designed — and find a way to make that fit in our world, to try and make the material feel real. To try to change the stripes on his torso into straps that would hold down his shoulder armor and hold the weight of the shield when he wore it on his back. To find ways to work it in so it doesn't necessarily feel as costume-y as it possibly could. That was one of the more exciting challenges to me, trying to make him feel real."

Concept art by Ryan Meinerding.

Said Meinerding, "Captain America's costume has an unabashedly extreme quality to it. It's red, white and blue, and proudly boasts stars and stripes. For those of us that love the character, that iconic, strong visual is part of what makes Cap so close to our hearts. We tried our hardest to keep that icon while allowing those not as familiar with the character to find him cool and appealing and not just shut down at the sight of such a powerfully poignant comic image. Relating his costume to a soldier's gear was a big step, and trying to use materials that would feel advanced for the 1940s was another part of that."

The film's producers also struggled to capture Captain America's essence as they hunted for the perfect actor to fill the iconic role. "If you look at our other films, you see that we cast performers first," Co-Producer Stephen Broussard said. "We make sure that we cast actors with real talent, with real acting chops, and that's certainly going to be the case with a character like Steve Rogers. It's a very complex character. He starts in one place, ends up in a completely different place, both physically and emotionally. You need someone that can play the broad range of that. You also need someone that when we get to *The Avengers* can go toe-to-toe with actors like Robert Downey Jr., can hold their own in a scene."

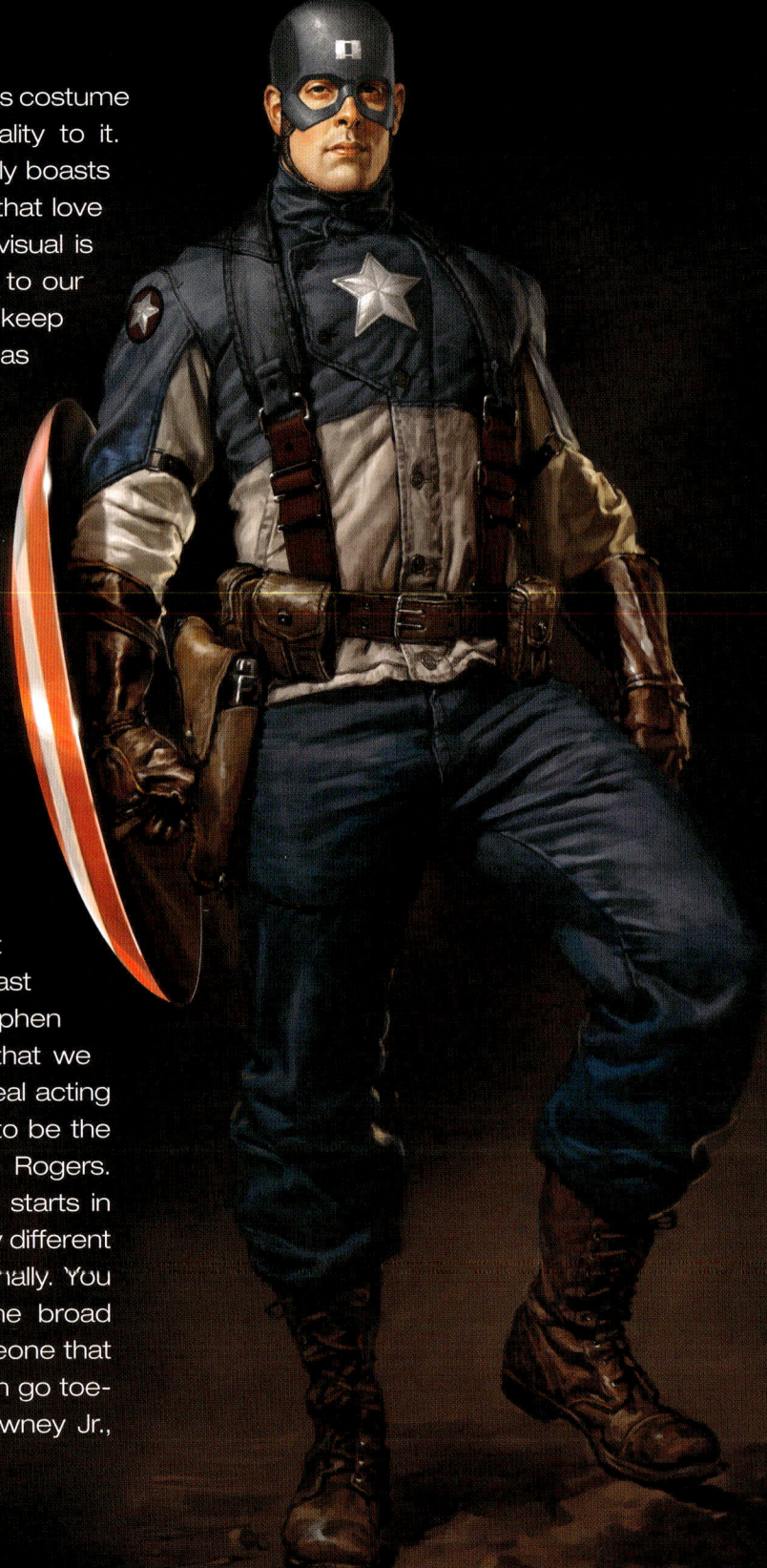

Concept art by Ryan Meinerding.

The role of the all-American hero eventually went to Chris Evans, an actor capable of the range required in Captain America's transformation. Said Evans, "I went and met with Joe and Kevin and Stephen, and they sat me down and gave a really good pitch of who this character was — and it's a pretty good story even independent of its super-hero aspect. It's about a guy who has a lot of shortcomings and who still chooses to not become jaded or bitter about it. He's a good man, an honest man, a noble man — and as a result of those virtues, he's given a gift. He's able to balance this new life he has with the old set of morals."

Concept art by Ryan Meinerding.

CAPTAIN AMERICA : FINAL

"The Captain America suit — the big finale suit — that went through a lot of different stages," Evans said. "Obviously, there are a lot of people involved in making the suit who worked very hard on it. I would just come in every couple weeks and try a new outfit on, and they would poke and prod and measure and cut, and I'd kind of stay out of it. Then, finally, they got it where they wanted it. And I think it looks fantastic."

Said Suit Modeler Paddy Whitaker, "The fabric for the suit is basically a ballistic nylon, which in fact is a heavy-duty woven nylon with a rubberized backing. It comes from a firm in the U.K., and we believe it's used for the manufacturing of horse blankets. But it's quite a tough material. The fabric is actually quite strong, more like a heavy denim or canvas."

Said Whitaker, "There were two ways of reading Ryan's drawing: It could either have been seen as sort of a puffy sort of satin — like a flight suit with padding — or more, something stronger. So the nylon definitely was interesting, though I also knew that nailing the right blue was going to be a big issue with the Cap suit. We actually chose a gray fabric quite deliberately because we knew that we could then push into various different blues and take it from there. So, yeah, it's come to quite a lot to get it to a stage where it's Cap fabric."

Concept art by Ryan Meinerding.

Production still.

In WWII, soldiers often had identifiable symbols painted on their helmets, and viewing Cap's signature wings in that light offered a grounding in the period.

Concept art by Ryan Meinerding.

The casting and costuming all came together in the end, and the result made the countless hours of hard work worthwhile. Said Meinerding, "For me, it's actually a really big sigh of relief. We went through so many different prototypes to see how it fit on him and how to make it look great on him and how to really make sure it was as good as it could be. So to see a version — where it actually feels big and it feels strong, and it feels like Captain America — it's been really exciting; it's been great."

Production still.

CHAPTER TWO
THE RED MENACE

Although *Captain America: The First Avenger* is primarily set during World War II, the filmmakers at Marvel Studios were quick to add a new twist to the concept of a period piece. Said studio head Kevin Feige, "Is this the authentic World War II period that you see on the History Channel? No, this is World War II of the Marvel Universe, where super-soldier programs are going on — where an organization called Hydra run by the Red Skull is tapping into these incredible sources of power, creating these vehicles and these weapons far beyond anything that we've seen before."

Said Co-Producer Stephen Broussard, "What's the Marvel version of that World War? What are the vehicles like? How do these powers clash in a way that's befitting of the time and of the character? So we're always looking for new and interesting ways to take existing bits of history and turn it on its ear."

And in that new past that never was, the biggest threat to world security wasn't the Nazi party, but an offshoot called Hydra — led by Captain America's most notorious villain, Johann Schmidt, the infamous Red Skull.

Keyframe art by Charlie Wen.

JOHANN SCHMIDT

"So the Schmidt you see in the beginning of the film looks a little bit like me," said Hugo Weaving, the actor charged with playing Captain America's nefarious foil. "My face is actually the mask that he wears, to get on in the world without having people in the world being horrified by the way he looks."

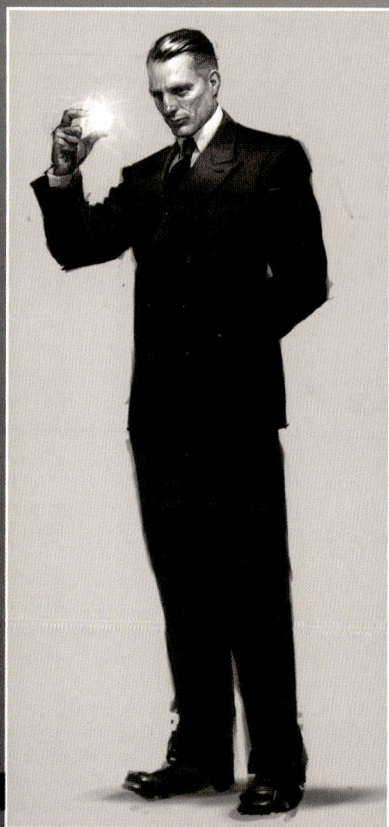

Concept art by Charlie Wen.

Concept art by Ryan Meinerding.

Concept art by Charlie Wen.

43

Production still.

JOHANN SCHMIDT'S OFFICE

With all of Hydra under his command, Schmidt seeks nothing less than complete and utter glory for himself. It's a character trait reflected in his impressive office, complete with a giant portrait of the Red Skull's ghastly visage.

Concept art by Mauro Borelli.

JOHANN SCHMIDT : NORWAY

Said Weaving, "He's a German officer, and we first meet him when he's hunting down this thing called the Tesseract, or the Cube. He's interested in Norse mythology, he's interested in the Aryan race, he's interested in Wagner. He's got all of these Germanic pretensions, I suppose, and an interest in a power beyond an Earthly power — so an interest in controlling this spiritual power, if you like. And I always thought that this was the most interesting thing about him as a character."

Concept art by Mauro Borelli.

Production still.

JOHANN SCHMIDT : CASTLE ROCK TOWER

Schmidt's interest in Norse lore leads him to the impressive Castle Rock Tower, a stone fortress that serves as the hiding place of the legendary Cosmic Cube. Fans of previous Marvel films may recognize the famous image of Yggdrasil — the World Tree, first glimpsed in *Thor* — on the bas-relief on the wall.

Concept art by Mauro Borelli.

Production still.

Said Production Designer Rick Heinrichs, "The depiction of the stone tower offered the opportunity to display the sheer physical power of Schmidt's Hydra Corps and their technology — specifically their massive tank the Landkreuzer, as it punches a hole in the side of the thick rock wall with its 'Fist of God' battering ram. The old stone walls give way to 20th-century technology as the new brutal might smashes the old building."

Concept art by Mauro Borelli.

Playing host to one of Hydra's early triumphs, Castle Rock Tower was meticulously designed by the *Captain America* art department. Said Heinrichs, "The sarcophagus of the Nordic king and the other funerary elements in the stone tower gave that set a dignified solemnity that heightens the shock and impersonality of the Hydra attack."

"We tied the design of the carved stone sarcophagus together with the Tree of Life bas-relief on the wall — researching historical motifs within the Nordic tradition, as well as other related cultures," Heinrichs said. "The complex, interwoven shapes were used by these earlier cultures as pictographic storytelling that explained the origins of the Earth. In this case, we wanted to connect the legend and mythology of the early Northern European culture and how that tradition perversely inspired the early nationalist yearnings that became Nazism."

Concept art by Mauro Borelli.

Production still.

Concept art by Mauro Borelli.

Production still.

Entombed at the heart of Castle Rock Tower is the Cosmic Cube, the object of the Red Skull's desire. Said Heinrichs, "In our movie, Red Skull takes the fascination with the mythology a step further to suggest that the Cosmic Cube is an ancient metaphysical power known to these early people and a part of the legends of their gods that he must possess at all costs."

Concept art by Mauro Borelli.

THE RED SKULL

"The Red Skull is the premier villain in the Captain America history," Broussard said. "He, in a lot of ways, is Steve Rogers' opposite. He went through the same process that transforms Steve Rogers into the super-soldier known as Captain America, but it went very wrong. He forced Dr. Erskine to put him through the procedure before it was ready; as a result, it left him disfigured, it left him scarred, but it did transform him into a super-soldier — into a stronger-than-normal human being."

60

Concept art by Charlie Wen.

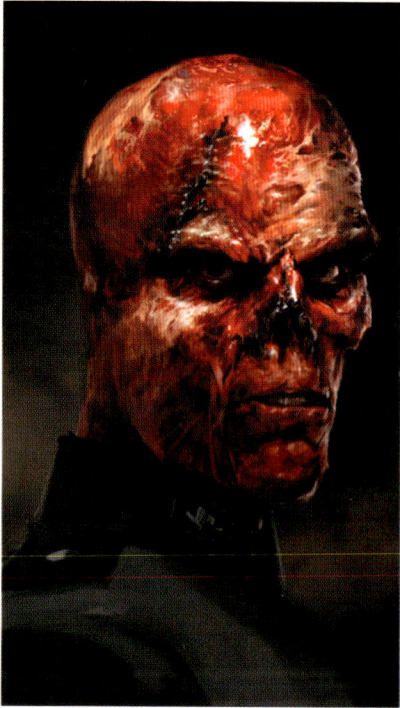
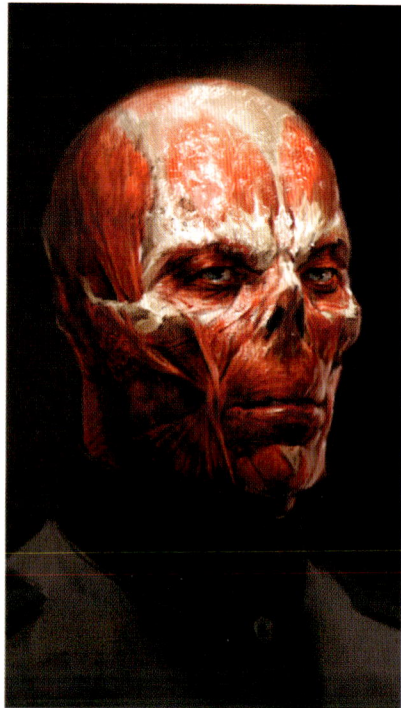
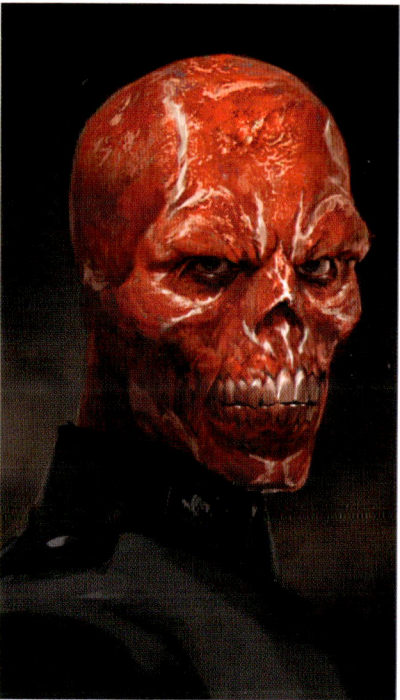
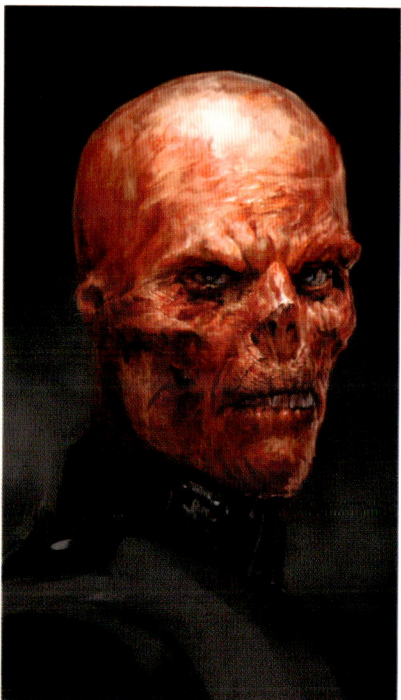

Said Broussard, "They're essentially brothers of the same father, and that provides us with some really cool thematic ground to explore. Our villains always work best when they are tied to our characters somehow, when they have a connection that extends beyond the fact they happen to be involved in the same conflict."

For the classic villain's design, Concept Artist Ryan Meinerding kept coming back to the iconic look of the comic-book version of the Red Skull. "We did a few versions, and it's pretty easy to go creepy with it because he could look burned, he could look scarred," Meinerding said. "I had done a version that at the time I was really excited about, and it was sort of very red with flecks of white to imply some skull, and it ended up feeling like a T-bone steak. So we definitely tried some different things and just ended up with the classic."

Concept art by Ryan Meinerding.

Said Concept Artist Charlie Wen, "Since my first priority on the film was to come up with the look of Hydra, it made sense to begin with the most recognizable element, Red Skull. When I first joined Captain America, Ryan had already done several iconic Red Skull head designs that kept the traditional appeal from the comics. I wanted to show other possibilities for his head that we could explore, from the more alien to a deformed look. Both directions strayed a bit too far from the iconic Red Skull of the comics, so we eventually went back to the more traditional look of his head.

"Some of these earlier Red Skull designs had a more operatic feel to them — a bit of pomp and circumstance, more focus on mixing different materials and textures — while the latter and final designs had less focus on larger textural changes and more emphasis on cleaner, more methodical lines and shapes with smaller textural shifts."

Concept art by Charlie Wen.

Concept art by Ryan Meinerding.

Production still.

Production still.

Production still.

After Meinerding designed the Skull's namesake, it was up to Wen to figure out the remainder of the twisted villain. Said Wen, "I was designing the rest of him, and I was looking at Nazi leaders. I was looking at the feel of some of the guys that were surrounding Hitler while trying to use some of the colors that Hitler had."

Production stills.

ARNIM ZOLA

For Arnim Zola, the filmmakers took a different approach than the comics, in which "he's a head in the TV screen in a big robot body," Screenwriter Stephen McFeely said. "So we decided to give that robot a backstory, and he is the Skull's right-hand man. And, as played by Toby Jones, he's just hilariously entertaining the whole time because he's sort of a witness to the over-the-top evil that's going on, and he's sort of the audience's eyes going like, 'Really, you're building a laser gun?'"

Concept art by Darrell Wagner, costume design by Anna B. Sheppard.

HYDRA TROOPERS

Knowing full well the Red Skull could only be as threatening as the army he commanded, the filmmakers put a great deal of thought in to creating the Hydra soldiers. "What we've suggested for this film is that like Luftwaffe and the SS were branches of the Nazi party, maybe there was a branch called Hydra that was in charge of advanced tech and deep science," Broussard said. "Throughout the course of the film, Schmidt becomes a little disgruntled — to say the least — because he gets this thing called the Comic Cube, which is essentially an energy source that allows him to take all the tech he had been building and take it even further — more impressive vehicles and weapons and planes. So suddenly, the arms race has shifted."

Concept art by Ryan Meinerding.

Said Meinerding, "The Hydra logo took a while to figure out. It might seem strange because of its similarity to the comics design, but we had a lot of trouble getting it approved. The comic version seemed a little too whimsical to the higher-ups, so I tried adding the suction cups to the tentacles and having the negative shapes they create read as gears. Since Hydra is all about advanced weaponry and machinery, the gear theme seemed to fit.

"The Hydra weapons were meant to be powered by the Cosmic Cube, so we went with the idea that each trooper had a cube battery pack on his back. The logic from there was that the only way to move that energy safely was to move it though rectilinear forms instead of cables. Only when the Cube power reaches the gun does it become weaponized, and that's where we used cylindrical forms. And of course, the blue energy from the Cube runs throughout all of the weapons."

Concept art by Ryan Meinerding.

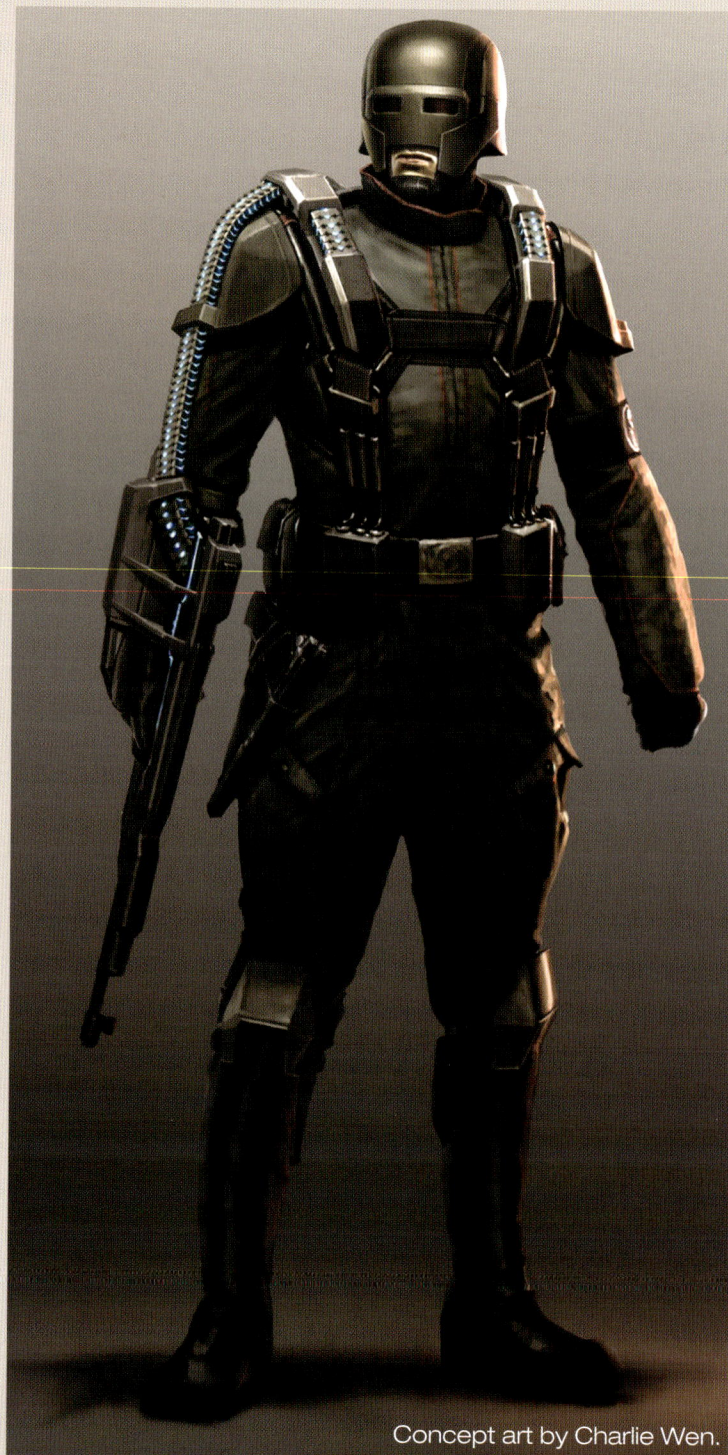

Concept art by Charlie Wen.

Said Richard Armitage, the actor who played Hydra agent Heinz Kruger, "Well, Hydra is sort of the experimental-weapons defense branch of the Nazi regime. So it's kind of top secret. I think most of the operatives will be working on a need-to-know basis. It's about experimental weapons, and that's something which opens a great line of research when you're really looking for the truth that this would have been based on. There was an arm of the Nazi party who were experimenting with really kind of revolutionary weapons and defense mechanisms."

Concept art by Ryan Meinerding.

Concept art by Charlie Wen.

Said Meinerding, "We had five classifications of Hydra soldiers: Infantry with a light weapon, Infantry with a heavy weapon, Flametrooper, Pilot and Motorcycle. They each had different variations to their helmet, weapons and costumes based on their function."

Concept art by Charlie Wen.

Concept art by Ryan Meinerding.

Concept art by Charlie Wen.

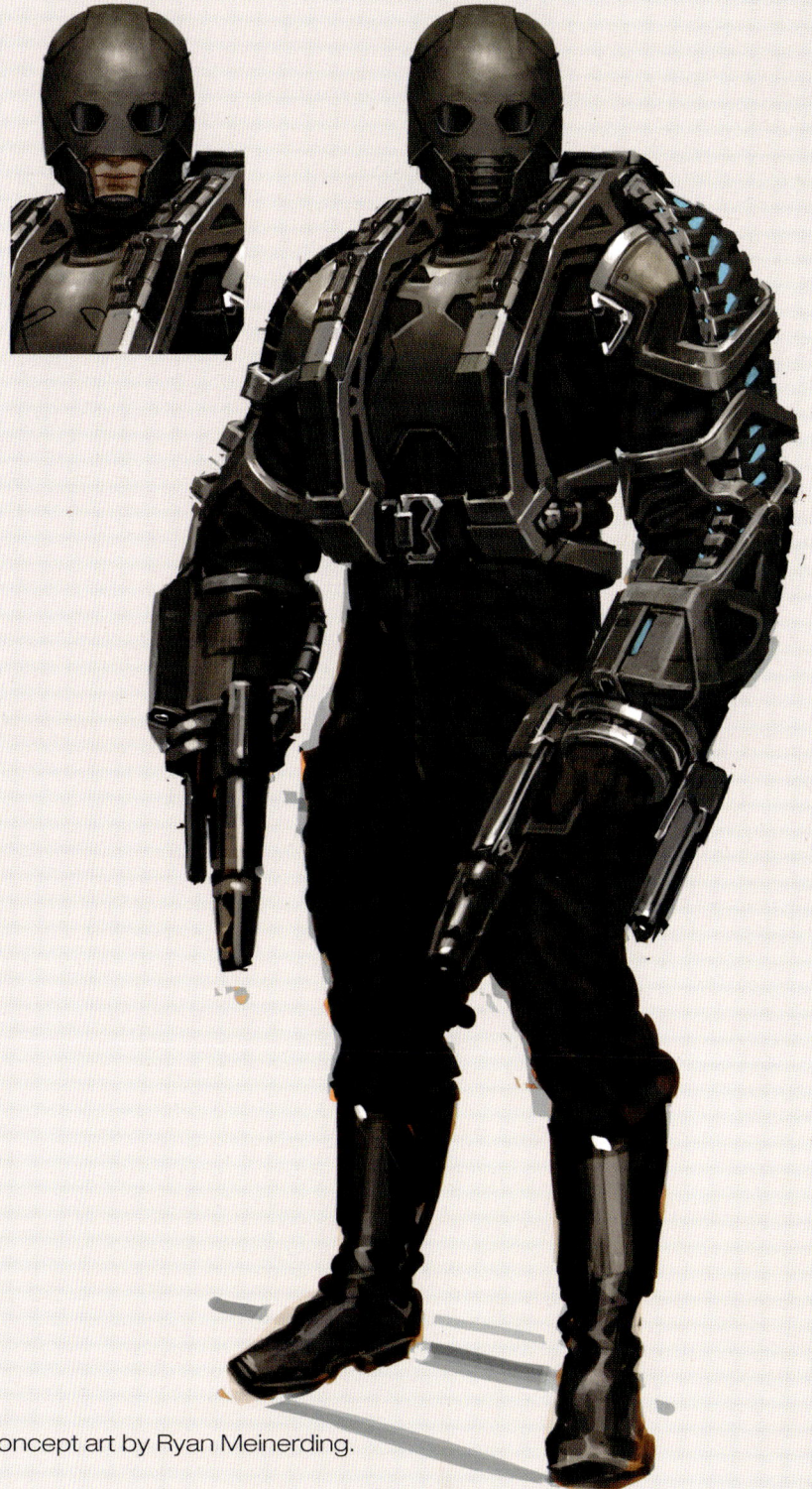

Concept art by Ryan Meinerding.

75

Concept art by
Ryan Meinerding.

Like every other part of the film, the creation of Hydra's uniforms and weaponry was a team effort. "Once the costume department nailed the pilot costume, it was really exciting to see," Meinerding said. "It has all of these hoses that run through it that are meant to be a pressure suit, similar to modern flight suits. They did a really great job with it."

Concept art by Charlie Wen.

Concept art by Ryan Meinerding.

"Joe has very distinct ideas about helmets and gear, and working with him on the design of Hydra and Cap was one of the great experiences of my career," Meinerding said. "Knowing that the man that designed Boba Fett trusted me with the design of some of his characters was truly an honor."

Because Hydra plays such a large role in the world of Marvel Comics, Meinerding and Wen wanted to be sure to pay tribute to the source material when appropriate. Said Meinerding, "A lot of the initial design takes were just trying to figure out how to include the signature 'H' from the comics. Once we realized we could use the Cube tech to be part of those straps and harnesses, it came together a bit more."

Said Wen, "Initially, I focused on a more low-tech machinery that was being powered by an extremely high-tech alien force. I tried to keep with the Industrial Age as much as possible to give greater emphasis to the era difference with the rest of the Marvel Universe, which is happening in present day. Eventually,

we gravitated back to a more high-tech version of the infantry and their armament. Ryan brought some of the high-tech back into Hydra with some amazing weapons that were extremely high-tech, yet still viable for the Marvel world in the WWII period.

"Designing infantry in any media is a different sort of animal to tackle. You are designing something that needs to work in groups small and large. Something I wanted to be sure of was that our Hydra soldiers were going to be strong enough to stand by themselves on the screen, but simple enough to work well with dozens on the screen at once. So some of the images I did were to make sure the design worked together when seen in a large group of repeating shapes, colors and materials."

Concept art by
Charlie Wen.

SLIGHTLY
BIGGER EYES

RM

Concept art by
Ryan Meinerding.

An important detail for the Hydra soldiers' overall look was their signature headgear. "I enjoyed designing the Hydra helmets most," Wen said. "All the helmets began with a thin cowl — much akin to the German pilot headgear of WWII, but with a decidedly Hydra take. The goggles slid along three metal pipings for each eye and attached on the sides to a rotation ring around the ears. An inner cowl was visible with replaceable mouth/nose pieces, depending on the purpose. I designed this for the base pilot, while other infantry that needed more protection were fitted with heavier helmets over this pilot base."

Said Meinerding, "Charlie really nailed the design of the Hydra helmets. They feel like the period, but definitely more sinister and threatening. And of course, they relate to the comic version of Hydra in strong way."

With each classification of Hydra soldier came new challenges for Meinerding and Wen. "With the Flame Trooper, the design challenge was how to integrate the Cube technology with a traditional flamethrower to make something that felt a little new," Meinerding said. "There were meant to be two triggers in the inner rings of the gun apparatus, and the trooper would rotate his hand to activate either the Cube weapon or the flamethrower."

Concept art by Charlie Wen.

Concept art by Ryan Meinerding.

HYDRA WEAPONS

Part of the fun for actor Hugo Weaving was using the Red Skull's various weapons. "The first gun you see Schmidt with is the classic Luger," Weaving said. "Once Schmidt gets hold of the Tesseract, or the Cube, and taps into the power with the help of Zola — his sort of scientist right-hand man — they manage to kind of harness the energy contained within this Cube. So Schmidt, Red Skull, then develops a Luger that is slightly more futuristic, but is powered by a miniature kind of Cube-powered battery. Anything to do with the Tesseract, or the Cube, has a blue light to it so that blue color kind of threads its way through all the scenes."

Concept art by Ryan Meinerding.

Concept art by
Ryan Meinerding.

Production still.

Production still.

Production still.

Concept art by Ryan Meinerding.

A major part of Hydra's overall look was determined by the high-tech weapons the organization employed, which were of particular interest to Director Joe Johnston. Said Meinerding, "The gun designs were specifically directed by Joe. He wanted them to look like technology first and a weapon second. After Paul Catlin had done a design based on a particle accelerator, we had the direction to go in."

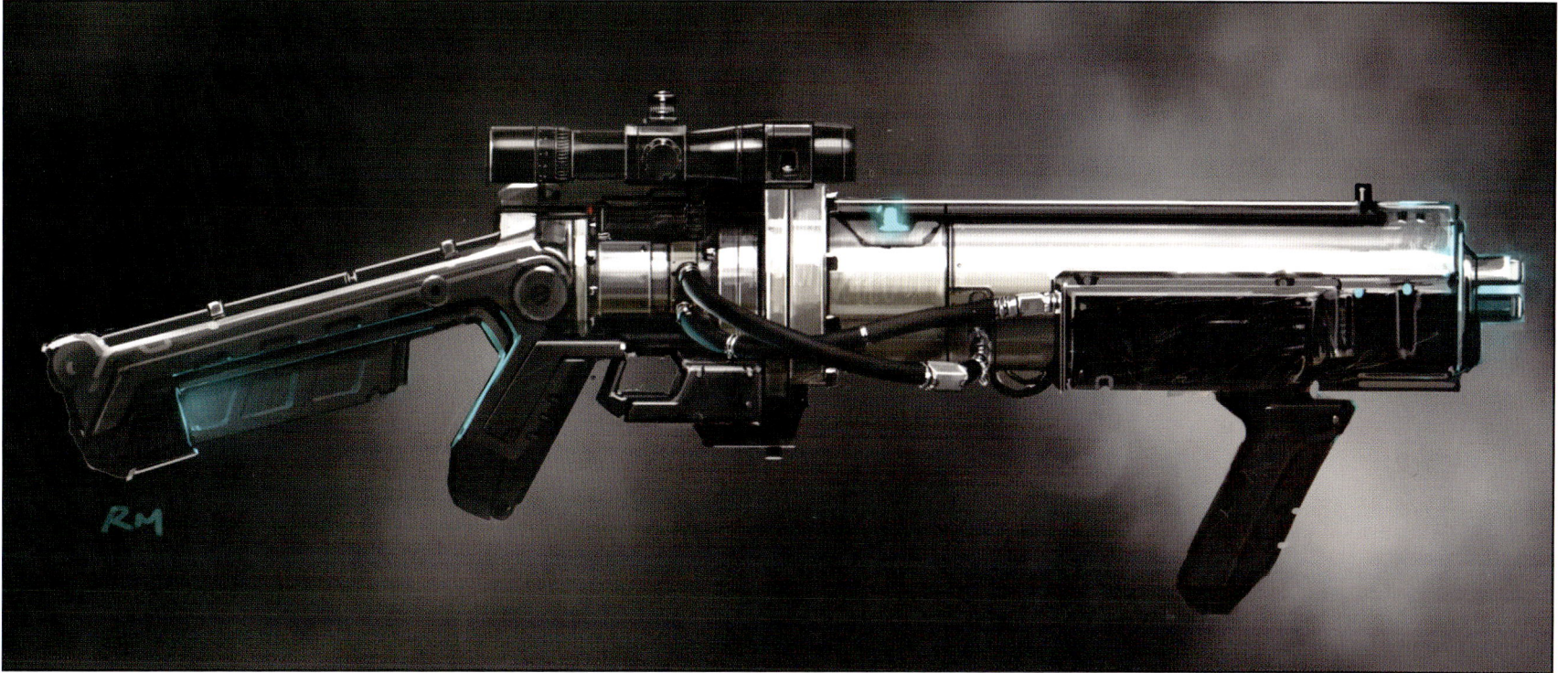

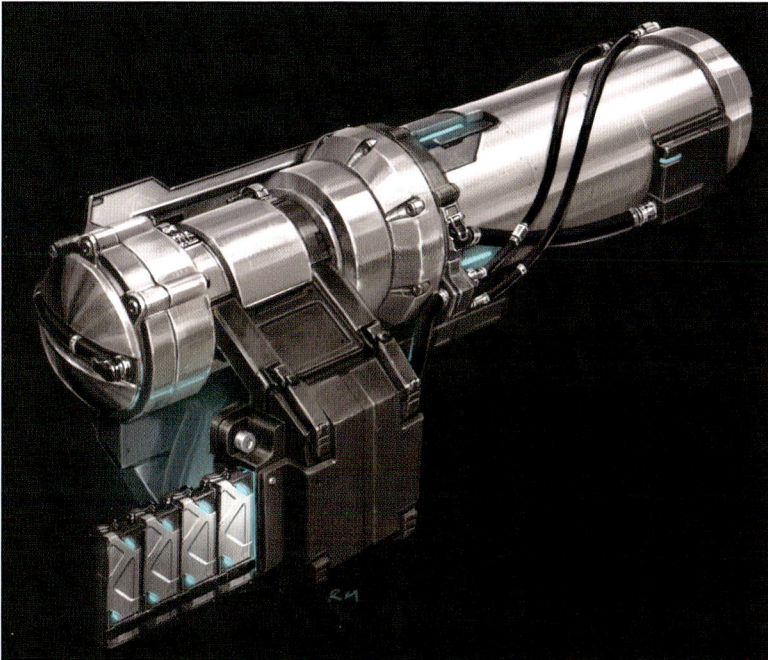

Production still.

Concept art by Ryan Meinerding.

HYDRA BASES

When crafting a home for the agents of this technological army, filmmakers were adamant about creating a unique combination of the real and the fantastic. Said Visual Effects Supervisor Christopher Townsend, "So our world is going to exist in this sort of slightly futuristic Marvel take on what the world will be, a retro future. So it's a future that could've been perceived in the '50s or in the '40s."

Concept art by Mauro Borelli.

"We're going to be shooting in various locations," Townsend said. "All the exterior stuff is shot elsewhere in Wales. And we're gonna be patching it all together. So hopefully, at the end of the day, you will believe you have gone from one world outside, which is supposed to be the foothills of the Alps in Europe, to inside the factory."

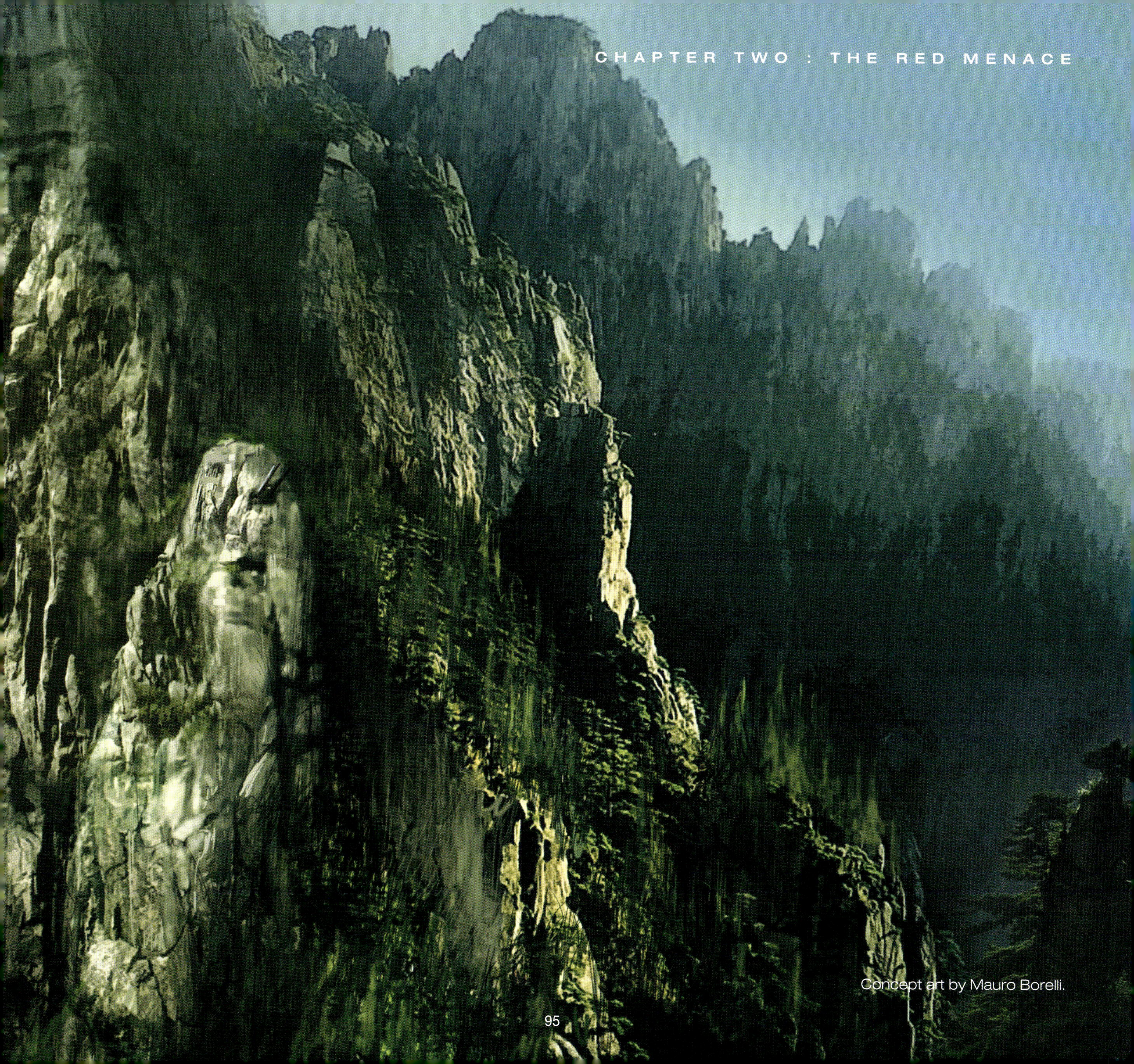

Concept art by Mauro Borelli.

Said Townsend, "There's some very organic shapes to Hydra. I think one of the art directors was saying that there's a lot of organic shapes of the skeletal structure in some of the buildings. If you had honey between two slices of bread and you pull them apart, you get that gooey, stretched, sort of organic thing. And that is the inspiration for the shapes, that sort of hollowing out of a structure as it's pulled apart. That's used a lot as our aesthetic within the movie for Hydra. It's very neat, very strong, very dramatic, very totemic — but it's more refined than what the Nazis were doing."

Said Heinrichs, "It was Joe's thought finally to throw out the clichéd 'bad guy's lair' idea and keep Hydra HQ hidden within the towering Alpine peaks, with only the windows of Schmidt's lab even remotely visible in the rocky Alpine carapace. All that remains to remind us of the turrets and castellation of the original idea is the natural 'architecture' of the mountains."

Concept art by Mauro Borelli.

To realize their futuristic version of the past, the filmmakers had to conduct their research differently than they would have for a traditional period piece. Said Townsend, "So rather than looking at '40s planes as our inspiration for our plane that we're creating, we're now looking at '50s planes. We're looking at '50s jet engines rather than '40s engine technology, that kind of stuff. So it's just a little bit more advanced than what was really there as a period piece — but again, very much grounded in reality. So hopefully, an audience will never be taken out of the real basis of the film."

Concept art by Mauro Borelli.

The challenge for Heinrichs and company for the Hydra bases again revolved around the idea of a retroactive future. "As we developed it, trying different versions to present Joe with a fresh concept, nothing was quite up to the task of how we wanted to present Schmidt's advanced technological and architectural aesthetic," Heinrichs said.

Concept art by Mauro Borelli.

Concept art by Jim Carson.

CHAPTER THREE

ALLIED FORCES

While Captain America may be an army of one, even he needs a little help to confront the futuristic threat of Hydra. To find a team worthy of backing up the American icon, the filmmakers had to look no further than Marvel's impressive library of war comics. And while some supporting characters, like Bucky Barnes and Peggy Carter, originated in Captain America's own title, others were taken from the pages of Marvel's most popular classic war comic: *Sgt. Fury and his Howling Commandos.*

Said Sebastian Stan, the actor who played Cap's right-hand man, Bucky Barnes, "The Howling Commandos are very crucial to the story. I think each of them in the comic books have very specific paths that they go on after their initial introduction. But in our story, they're crucial because they're those guys you identify with or you learn about. They have a certain way of speaking. They're real people that are brought together by war, and they've survived a lot and they've just been through a lot."

Said Co-Producer Stephen Broussard, "It was sort of Marvel's Dirty Dozen going through these World War II period adventures. You had characters like Gabe Jones and Dum Dum Dugan taking out Hitler and his bad guys in many missions throughout the time period. We saw it as an opportunity to give Cap a team — so that he's not just out on the field alone, but he's able to surround himself with these people with special skills."

With the Commandos at his side and the rest of his allies in the Strategic Scientific Reserve helping him along the way, Captain America is ready to go from playing hero to becoming one.

Keyframe art by Ryan Meinerding.

PEGGY CARTER

Said Broussard, "All great Marvel love interests, all great female leads in Marvel movies, are full-blooded characters in and of themselves. Our female characters do not just show up and bat their eyelashes. That's always a boring sort of damsel-in-distress model that does not work, so we always want the women in our movies to be just as strong as the men. And a lot of times, they're the ones that define our men, that help them understand who they are. And that's certainly the case in *Captain America*. The love interest is a woman named Peggy Carter, who's there in the beginning. She's working in the Super-Soldier Program. She's a beautiful woman, but she's also very strong and capable."

Peggy Carter
Nº 1

Concept art by Darrell Wagner,
costume design by Anna B. Sheppard.

Portrayed by actress Hayley Atwell, Peggy Carter plays a vital role in the film. Her wardrobe — although subtler than the bold red, white and blue uniform worn by Captain America — nevertheless had to set her apart from the rest of the cast. Said Atwell, "It was very important for Anna Sheppard, the costume designer on this, to come up with a series of costumes that were of its time and practical for Peggy given her position, but also made her stand out as the love interest and the female lead. And making her have an element of glamour was also very important for the 1940s woman. Members of my family at the time were putting their hair into rollers the night before and not leaving the house without lipstick."

Concept art by Darrell Wagner, costume design by Anna B. Sheppard.

Production still.

COLONEL PHILLIPS

Finding the right actor to play Peggy Carter's boss, and Captain America's commanding officer, was not a decision the filmmakers made lightly. Their search ended with noted actor Tommy Lee Jones. Said Chris Evans, "He's an icon. I grew up watching his stuff. He's fantastic. After all these years and all these movies and all these accomplishments, he just comes to work. He's professional. He has no attitude; he's not a diva. He does whatever is asked of him, he knows his lines, he knows what he's doing. He's giving and supportive, and he treats everyone with respect. It's just an amazing way to be."

Production still.

Concept art by James Hegedus.

Concept art by Ryan Meinerding.

STRATEGIC SCIENTIFIC RESERVE

"The SSR logo was a way of unifying the modern S.H.I.E.L.D. logo with its 1940 counterpart using the eagle symbol, as well as using the eagle's wing as a symbol for Cap's helmet and the Invaders," Concept Artist Ryan Meinerding said.

HOWARD STARK

Casting Howard Stark — the father of Tony Stark, a.k.a. Iron Man — was another challenging opportunity. Said Broussard, "With Howard Stark being in the *Captain America* film specifically, I think that was one that we thought about for a long time, because it makes sense. In the comics, he was around in World War II; he did work on the Manhattan project. He was very much modeled after a Howard Hughes character, a private arms manufacturer that did help the Allies win the war effort. And we have an opportunity to go back and tell the history of characters that people already know — to delve back into that and to make it richer and to see where these people come from, who their parents are, how their stories lead right back to the people in this movie and vice versa."

Concept art by Darrell Wagner, costume design by Anna B. Sheppard.

Production still.

For Howard Stark, the filmmakers decided on Dominic Cooper, recognizing in the actor the ability to convey the trademark Stark charisma established so well by Robert Downey Jr. in the *Iron Man* films. Said Atwell, "Howard Stark is this slightly slimy, suave kind of Clark Gable-looking dude who is someone who is ahead of his time. And he's quite brilliant, but gets it wrong quite a lot. But that adds an element of danger in his work."

Concept art by Darrell Wagner, costume design by Anna B. Sheppard.

Production still.

THE HOWLING COMMANDOS

A broad mix of characters, the Howling Commandos serve as Captain America's field team. Meinerding helped shape the squad's look, a challenging task as each member required unique and original design elements. Said Meinerding, "Designing Morita involved trying to figure out how to weave a high-tech looking radio throughout his costume so he could be the Howling Commandos communications officer. I ended up using a more modern top to a military radio as reference.

"Falsworth's design is probably the most layered because we were subtlety trying to work the Union Jack onto his chest by using the straps and webbing to hint at the comic character Union Jack. We did try and work in the more typical British military uniform with him, but definitely added some custom elements.

"Dernier was a French Resistance fighter, and we decided to make him a bomb expert. We designed his costume and webbing to hold landmines and a few types of grenades.

Concept art by Ryan Meinerding.

Concept art by Andrew Williamson.

Production still.

Said actor Kenneth Choi, who played Commando Jim Morita, "What they've done for the film is a cross-section of some of the characters from the comic-book mythology. So they have Captain America, Bucky and Union Jack from the Invaders, and they mixed them with characters who are members of the Howling Commandos — like Dum Dum Dugan; Gabe Jones; my character, Morita; and Jacques Dernier."

Production still.

JAMES "BUCKY" BARNES

Bucky was another difficult role to cast, Broussard said. "He is the sidekick, but there's also some places that he goes to in the Marvel Universe — not necessarily in this movie — that we need to leave open to possibility if we decide to explore the character further. And Sebastian was someone that we weren't that familiar with, but our casting director brought him to our attention.

"What's creative about a guy like Bucky is that he's always liked Steve from the beginning, when he was a 98-pound weakling. They grew up together, so with a character like this you can trace Steve's journey. He's the guy that can see Steve when he was young, see Steve after he transforms, can comment on the guy he sees he's become and, quite frankly, can check Steve when he gets full of himself and can say, 'You're getting a little too much ego here, a little too much of a swollen head.'"

Said Meinerding, "Bucky was a fun challenge. The script definitely called for more of a dark, harder-edged character than the boy sidekick from the original comics. We tried to find a balance that still harkened to the character with the buttons on his coat, but to make him a bit more grown-up. Hopefully, it feels like a period costume that is more slightly advanced for a skilled sniper."

Production still.

TIMOTHY "DUM DUM" DUGAN

The comic-book companion to Nick Fury, Dum Dum Dugan makes his Marvel movie debut here. As played by actor Neal McDonough, Dugan's character even inspired some of his fellow actors. Said Kenneth Choi, "When you see Dum Dum Dugan's costume, I mean it's pretty fantastic. And he looks just like Dum Dum Dugan. So it absolutely puts you in the feel of being in World War II, but at the same time being a part of this Marvel Universe."

The art department agreed McDonough was the right choice for the part. "Once McDonough was cast, Dum Dum was very straightforward to design," Meinerding said. "He brings so much to the character that all we had to do was give him a costume that could emphasize his barrel chest and strong stance, throw in the signature bowler hat, and Dum Dum came to life."

Concept art by Ryan Meinerding.

CHAPTER FOUR
THE BATTLE LINES

To ground *Captain America: The First Avenger* firmly in reality, the filmmakers realized the world the story takes place in would be every bit as important as the characters inhabiting it. Tasked with fleshing out that world were Director Joe Johnston and Production Designer Rick Heinrichs.

But the film's painstaking detail wasn't just for the audience's benefit. The actors also found inspiration in the scenery. Said JJ Feild, who portrayed Montgomery Falsworth of the Howling Commandos, "Everything is big. The scale is phenomenal. You read a script and it says, 'Red Skull's Command Center' or 'The Headquarters' or 'The Soldiers' Camps,' and you imagine a nice sort of cheated set somewhere. No, they went and built them. I mean, it seems that the possibility to create whatever the writers and Marvel have imagined is endless.

"They just build them, and we get to bounce off the walls and destroy everything. The sets are all beautiful, and then we come swinging through windows and destroy everything."

Keyframe art by Ryan Meinerding.

WORLD'S FAIR

One of the film's first scenes takes place at the World's Fair, which proved to be a great chance for Heinrichs and company to delve into the idyllic America of the past. "I loved the fact that with the World Exposition of Tomorrow, we got to present the American optimism about the future as a national characteristic," Heinrichs said. "Here, we see that technology can lead to a brighter, happier future that democratically advances everyone on the path to peace and prosperity. In contrast, the future presented by Hitler and the Nazis was one of subjugation, oppression and misery — with advancement only for the most merciless and cunning. Never has the contrast between opposing forces been so delineated: humanism vs. totalitarianism. We embraced the opportunity to tell that story visually, particularly with Howard Stark's enthusiastically creative entrepreneurship."

Concept art by Henrick Tamm.

While moviegoers first glimpsed a contemporary version of the pavilion in *Iron Man 2*, the World's Fair in *Captain America* had to reflect a more retro feel. Said Visual Effects Supervisor Christopher Townsend, "We then have a Marvel pavilion in the 1940s, so how do we tie in that aesthetic of what we have in a contemporary world with our '40s Marvel pavilion, which is where the Marvels expo exists? It is trying to find that sort of art-nouveau, art-deco inspired world that we have in those beautiful shapes and round, smooth surfaces."

Production still.

Concept art by Henrick Tamm.

RECRUITMENT CENTER

An important plot point in the film, the World's Fair's Recruitment Center reminds the audience how important the idea of fighting for his country is to Steve Rogers, despite his physical shortcomings holding him back. Rogers isn't even tall enough to see his face reflected on the body of an average soldier.

DO YOU SEE YOURSELF IN THIS MAN'S ARMY?

ENLIST T

Concept art by Henrick Tamm.

Production still.

131

Production still.

REBIRTH LAB

While crafting Captain America was a challenge for all involved, creating his alter ego — the frail Steve Rogers — proved just as difficult. Said Special Effects Supervisor Christopher Townsend, "What we're trying to turn him into is the 98-pound weakling and make him shorter and thinner — remove the muscles from his neck, his shoulders, his chest and all that kind of stuff. So we're literally skinny-ing him down, and it's very exciting from a visual-effects point of view of how we're going about that."

The goal was to create an effect that didn't look like an effect. "He's now small, but they won't really think about it too much," Townsend said. "It will just be, 'Hey, Chris Evans is a small guy. I thought he was big.' And then in the transformation, 'Yeah, there he is. That's the Chris Evans that people know.'"

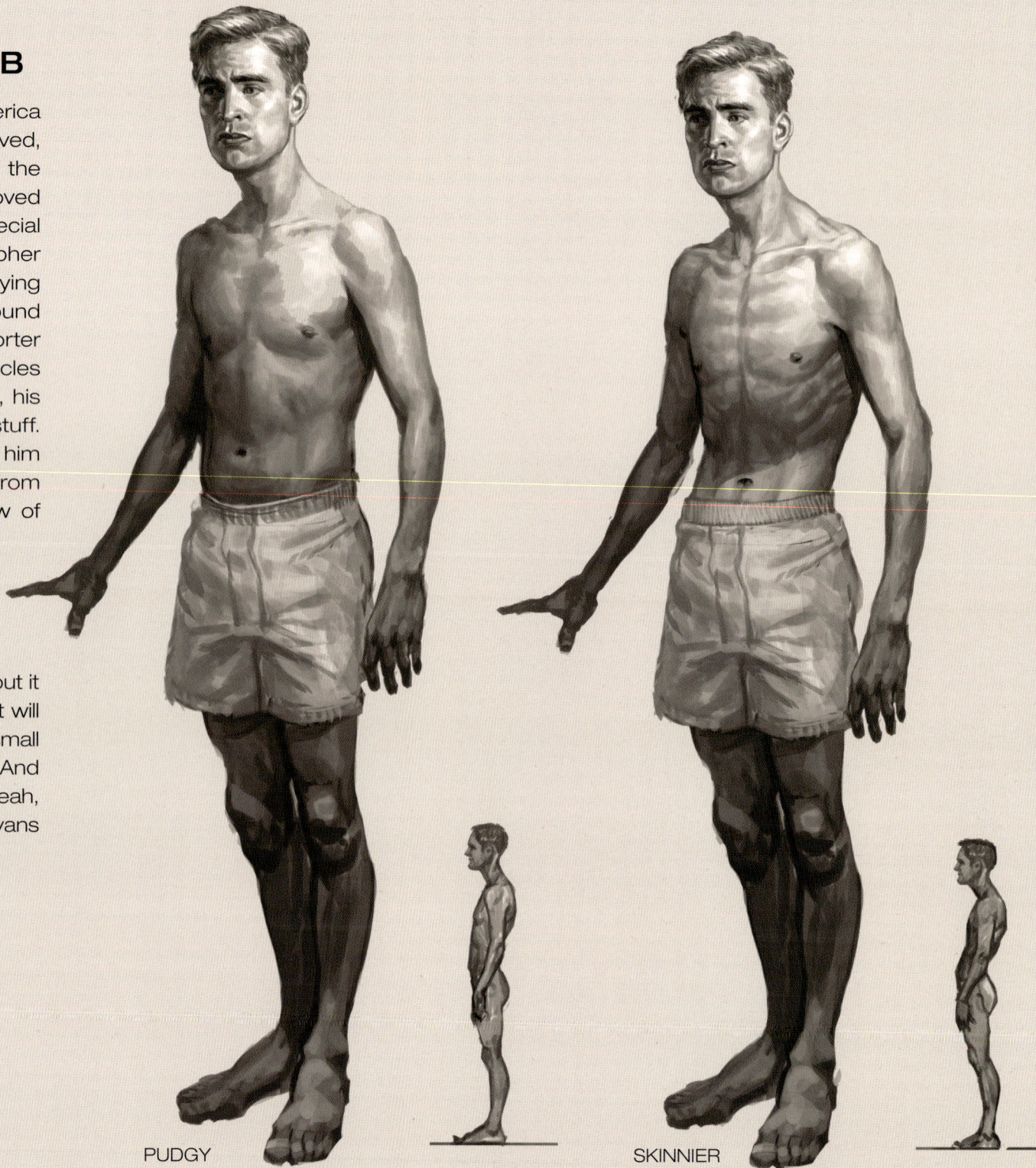

Concept art by Ryan Meinerding.

PUDGY

SKINNIER

134

EMACIATED AND
HUNCHED A LOT

Production still.

Another impressive set crafted by Heinrichs and crew, the Operation Rebirth Lab was a favorite of many of the actors. Said Leander Deeney, the visual-effects body double for scrawny Steve Rogers, "The set was brilliant. The way the design had been achieved of making it look like a kind of beautiful retro design. There's this very weird shade of green on everything. Everything was just brilliant, completely brilliant."

Computer-generated set by Paul Castling.

Steve Rogers double Leander Deeney shooting the Rebirth sequence.

Production still.

Home to one of the most important scenes in the film, the Operation Rebirth Lab is vital to the origin of Captain America. Said Producer Kevin Feige, "Right in the middle of World War II, as Oppenheimer was working on the Manhattan Project, there was another project going on, which was called Operation Rebirth — the Super-Soldier Program. It revolved around the belief that someone's potential could be unlocked with science, so that they could operate at the pinnacle of human achievement. Take any gold medalists from the Olympics, up it by about 10 percent, put it all into one person — that's what the Super-Soldier needs to be. And they think the future of the war relies on it."

Concept art by Ryan Meinerding.

139

NEW YORK CITY

When searching for a location to film the exterior scenes that needed to pass as 1940s Brooklyn, the art department had to overcome many hurdles to achieve the desired look. Said Co-Producer Stephen Broussard, "We had quite a tough time actually finding a section of street that worked for the city, for New York — let alone for period New York, because the architecture is so distinct from the time period. But Rick Heinrichs has done an amazing job turning the street completely different from when we visited it into what it is now."

Concept art by Ryan Meinerding.

Concept art by Henrick Tamm.

Concept art by Mauro Borelli.

ALLIED HQ

"I was deeply affected by my visit to Churchill's War Rooms in the center of London," said Heinrichs, remembering his influences for the Allied Headquarters. "I found the idea that the ultimately successful conduct of the war and defense of Britain had to be strategized within the modest warren-like basement of a government building there, and that the chief participants had to do their critical work living in such a severely circumscribed manner, to be a lesson in humility and the perseverance of the human spirit against tyranny. This felt like the spirit of Captain America."

Said Heinrichs, "The Allied HQ for our film needed to feel subterranean and hidden, but also workmanlike — a think-tank with all the advantages of state-of-the-art communications, mapping and strategic planning facilities. The bricked arches and under-crofting reinforce the impression of stoic Allied resistance. The warmer colors of the uniforms and environment contrast with the cold Hydra/Nazi aesthetic."

Computer-generated set by Nathan Schroeder.

OPERATIONS
MAP

UNDERWOOD

WHIP AND FIDDLE PUB

A place usually dedicated to relaxation and camaraderie, the Whip and Fiddle Pub is the Army's favorite bar. Its destruction during the film serves as a reminder of exactly how serious a business war truly is.

Concept art by Mauro Borelli.

Production still.

In stark contrast to the color palette and earthier feel of the Allied camps, the world the Red Skull and Hydra inhabit proved equally challenging for Heinrichs and his team. Said Heinrichs, "The Hydra Headquarters, Schmidt's secret lab and the Hydra Base housing the revolutionary Orbital Bomber had to have a unique yet appropriate look. The Hydra technology and the architecture that houses it wanted to feel cutting-edge within our context — perversely designed as an innovatively streamlined and efficient, but deadly effective, force."

Concept art by Adam Brockbank.

Still of Hugo Weaving on set prior to digital nose removal.

ZOLA'S LAB

Said Heinrichs, "We chose metallic surfaces and a cold color scheme to describe Schmidt's basic inhumanity, but also to convey the sense of superior science. The Nazis had some very innovative weapons programs in development, which the end of the war in 1945 thankfully brought to an end."

Concept art by Mauro Borelli.

SCHMIDT'S LAB

"Our conceit was to consider Hydra the progenitor of those programs," Heinrichs said. "And in our imaginations, Schmidt and Zola brought the historical research into the realm of plausible science fiction. Behind the smooth, metallic surfaces, though, hides a twisted, disfigured monster."

Concept art by Mauro Borelli.

CHAPTER FIVE
HEAVY ARTILLERY

By creating a Marvel version of the 1940s, Director Joe Johnston and Production Designer Rick Heinrichs were able to put their vivid imaginations to use in ways impossible in a standard period piece. And nowhere in the film is that more apparent than the design of the props and vehicles. From the futuristic Cosmic Cube to Cap's iconic shield, the art department took special care in creating ultra-sophisticated period weaponry.

For the many impressive Hydra vehicles destined to share the spotlight with the film's cast, Johnston and Heinrichs looked to Lead Vehicle Designer Daniel Simon to craft equipment that fit the time period, but also appeared more advanced than anything that would have existed during that bygone era.

Said Simon, "Joe's knowledge of period vehicles is extensive, and together we would flip through tons of books, magazines and websites to find ideas of how the Hydra technology should look on screen. It was just a question of how far we would push the look of Hydra."

Keyframe art by Ryan Meinerding.

CAPTAIN AMERICA'S SHIELD

Captain America's uniform may be an important part of his presence, but any comic-book fan will tell you it's the shield that makes the man. Cap's weapon of choice, used both offensively and defensively, is arguably the film's most important prop. Said Prop Master Barry Gibbs, "The team that worked with me took the initial designs that came back from 1942, and we extended them. We adapted it to modern times. Effectually, it went from a very plain shield to something that's kind of a little bit more high-tech."

Concept art by Ryan Meinerding.

When the Army finally decides to put Captain America's unique talents to good use, Howard Stark designs a variety of prototype shields for Steve Rogers before stumbling upon the perfect model. A seeming contradiction combining both simplicity and advanced technology, the shield just needed a patriotic paint job to be ready for action.

Howard Stark's Captain America shield prototypes, concept art by Paul Castling.

Production still.

THE COSMIC CUBE

Another fondly remembered object from the comics that plays a pivotal role in *Captain America: The First Avenger* is the legendary Cosmic Cube, which tips the balance of power during World War II in favor of the forces of Hydra under the Red Skull. Said Co-Producer Stephen Broussard, "The Cosmic Cube is basically this very powerful energy source that our villain, the Red Skull, has used to harvest and make amazing planes and weapons and lasers — and could even have grander possibilities with it once he figures out how to use it in a way that's very scary and very real and makes this very much in the Marvel Universe."

Concept art by Ryan Meinerding.

The Cosmic Cube in the film is similar in many ways to its four-color predecessor, but Broussard pointed to at least one notable difference. "It's always important to us to explore the things that fans enjoy and that have been huge, fun things in the comics forever. There's always a need to adapt and change a little bit for purposes of our movie. In the comics, the Cosmic Cube was this omnipotent device that if you thought it, it had happened. Obviously, if you give your bad guy that, it's a little too powerful."

Concept art by Ryan Meinerding.

Concept art by Ryan Meinerding.

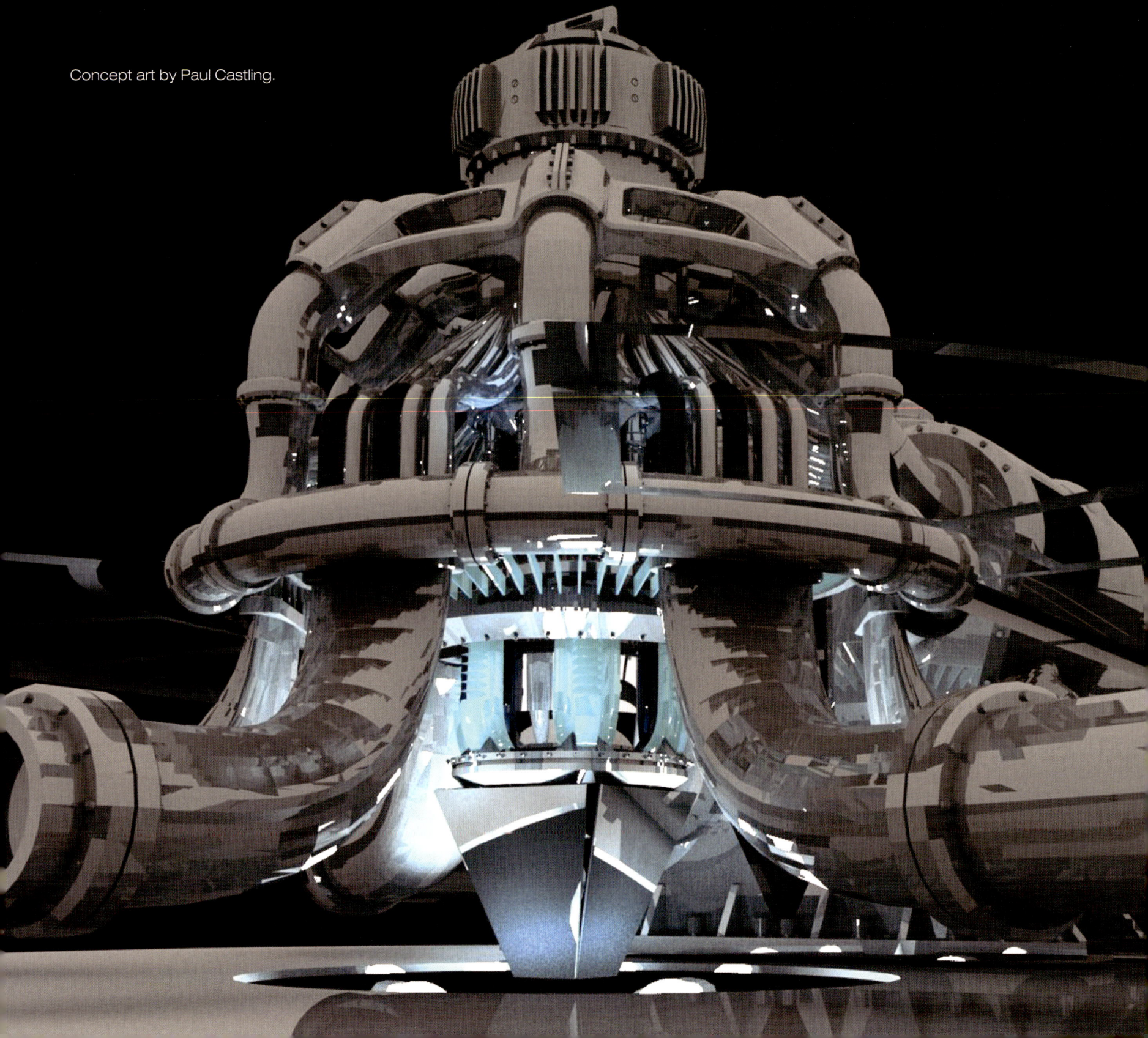

With the Cosmic Cube in its possession, Hydra has a new power source that alters the mechanics of its vehicles and therefore changes the appearance of an everyday engine or cradle. Said Simon, "We studied what was possible back then and took it just ten percent further, not more. That's enough to make the Hydra people look really evil and ahead. We studied propulsion technology, materials, car design, color schemes, etc. It was a gearhead's dream to professionally research any kind of technical detail of this very innovative time period."

Concept art by Daniel Simon.

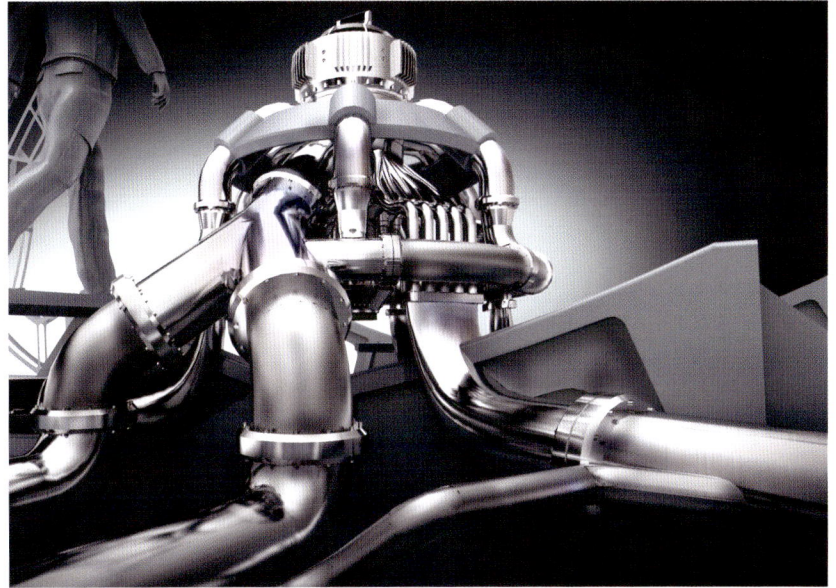

HYDRA WEAPONRY DESIGNS

"Our final designs reflect a fictive vision of what an advanced German design task force could have come up with in 1940, but stay truthful to the established Marvel Universe," Simon said. "We didn't want to go sci-fi. It was more like if you would manipulate our designs into a blurry black-and-white photograph, you could make historians think they discovered an unknown, but real, WWII experiment.

"I am coming from a background of professional car design, and historical vehicles always impressed me. They are so exotic just because they were made before my time, I cannot relate to them — yet they thoroughly fascinate me. Recreating such machinery on a fantasy level for a feature film is a dream for anybody with my interests."

- Ink Jet Vellums
- Ink Jet Bonds
- Color Bonds

Contact your local Clearprint deal

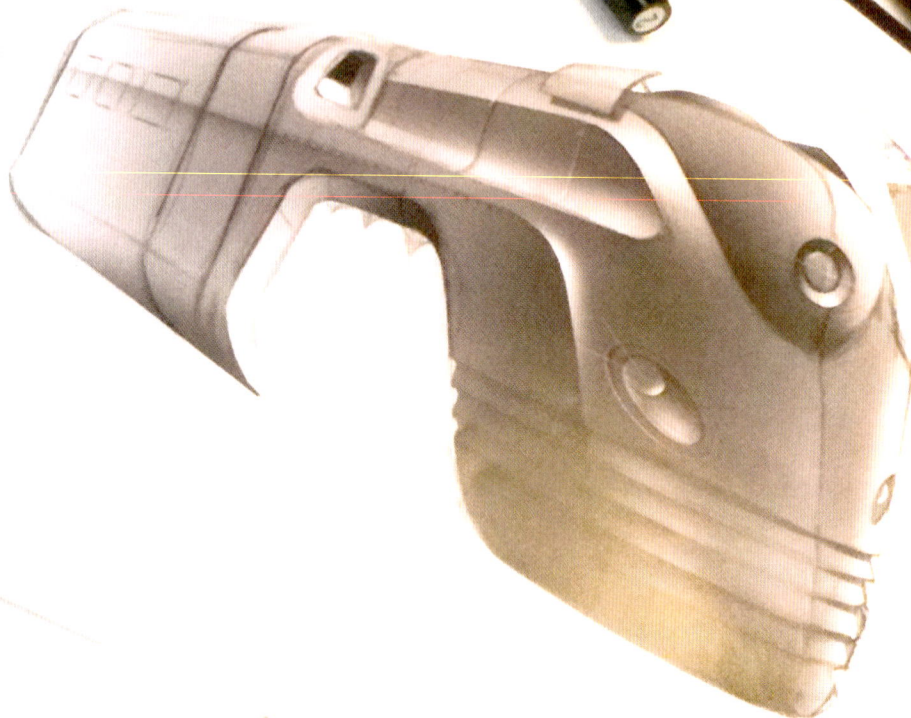

Daniel Simon works on Hydra vehicle designs in the Marvel Studios Pre-Production offices.

JOE, RICK, KEVIN, STEPHEN, JOHN,
THANK YOU FOR THIS
UNIQUE EXPERIENCE.

ALL THE BEST, DANIEL SIMON
LOS ANGELES, 2010

Daniel Simon's thank-you note to crew members.

HYDRA UBER TANK

Simon began his work on *Captain America: The First Avenger* with the large Hydra tank, striving for a design that hadn't been seen before in film. Said Simon, "The sheer size that was given by the story forced me to create a unique silhouette to avoid the feel of a ridiculous, scaled-up tank. It had to have its own believable aesthetic."

The bulk of the tank was necessary when its firepower was taken into consideration. "A forward-angled tread layout and a stubby turret nestled between the highest point of the tread seemed to work," Simon said. "That concept transported visually the massive structure of the vehicle necessary to fire those huge rounds."

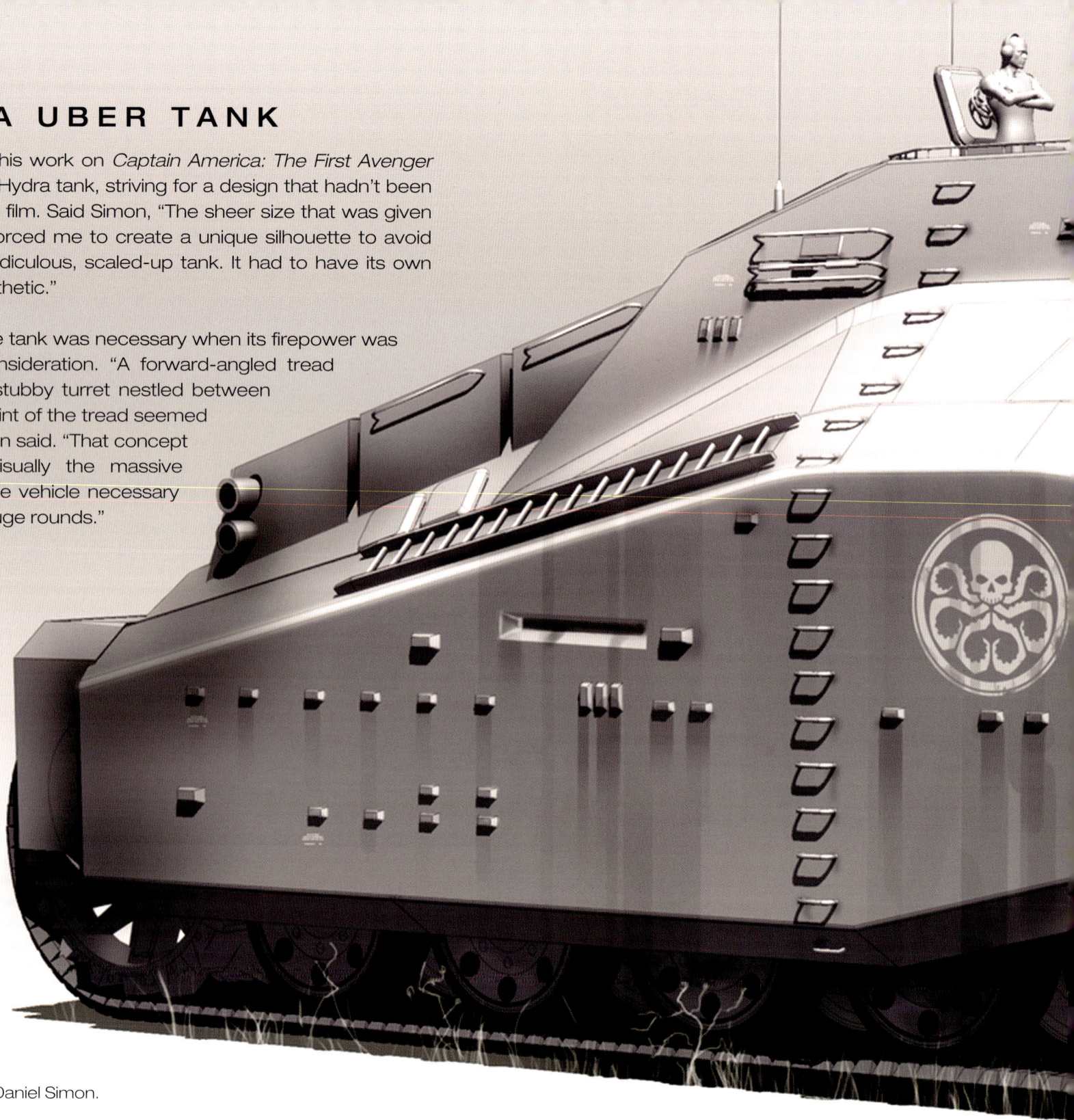

Concept art by Daniel Simon.

CAPTAIN AMERICA
HYDRA TANK ARMORED CONCEPT

EXTRA TURRET ON TOP CAN TURN

SMALL OFF-CENTER CONTROL BRIDGE

DETAILS FOR SCALE

MAIN GUN NESTLED BETWEEN TREADS FOR BETTER STRUCTURE

OPEN SIDE WITH UTILITY RACKS

REMOTE SIDE TURRETS

FULLY ENCLOSED BACK SIDE

THIN BARREL REDUCES FIRE TIME TO TWO SHOTS PER MINUTE. FOR THE EXTREME SPEED AMMUNITION WAS NO FASTER MECHANISM IN PLACE YET

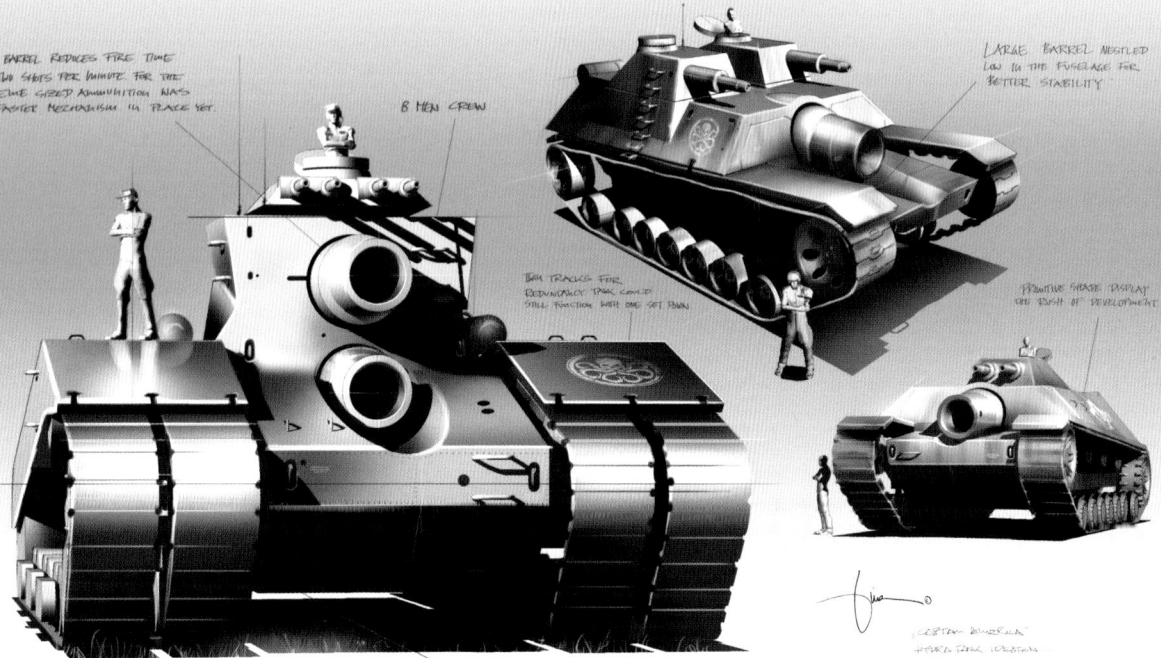

8 MEN CREW

LARGE BARREL NESTLED LOW IN THE FUSELAGE FOR BETTER STABILITY

TWIN TRACKS FOR REDUNDANCY TANK COULD STILL FUNCTION WITH ONE SET DOWN

PRIMITIVE SHADE DISPLAY OBD RUSH OF DEVELOPMENT

Designing the Hydra tank was a process of trial and error. Early ideas of a massive twin gun, required because of an imaginary long reloading time, fell through," Simon said. "Another dropped idea was automatic guns in the side skirts. Instead, we went for an additional mini-turret in the front, at that time the only movable weapon on the vehicle.

With every design stage, the wheels got covered more and more by integrated side skirts, but I left the front wheel exposed to at least see some wheel movement. The angle of the side skirts repeating on top and bottom show our attention to detail and proportion. The offset wheel arrangement on the tank is a detail that Joe Johnston requested, knowing that this is a typical German tank feature."

Concept art by Daniel Simon.

171

Concept art by Ryan Meinerding, vehicle design by Daniel Simon.

173

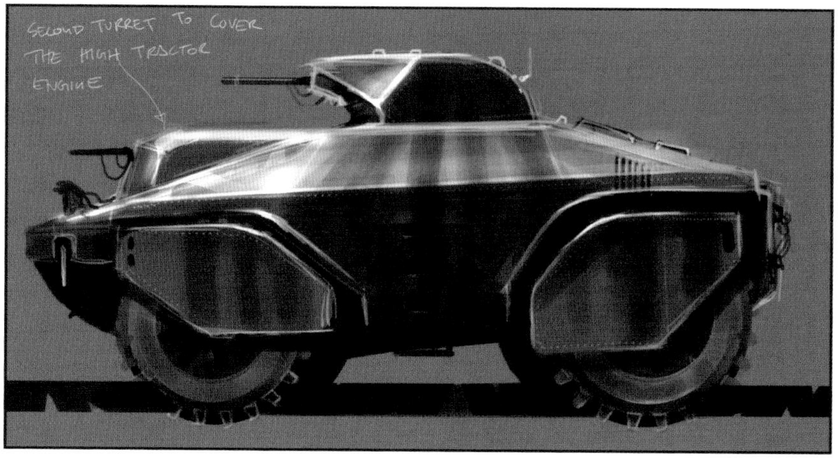
SECOND TURRET TO COVER
THE HIGH TRACTOR
ENGINE

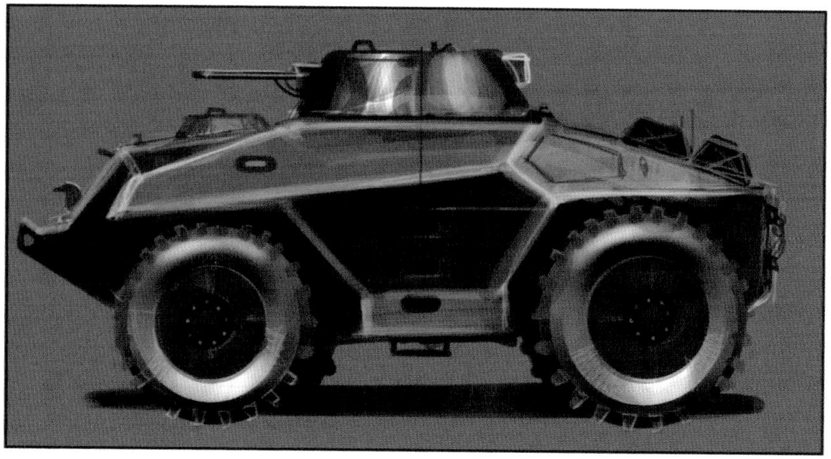

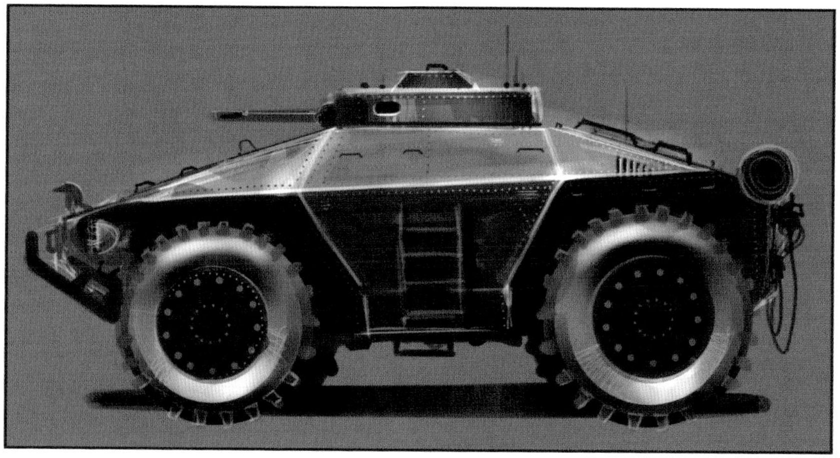

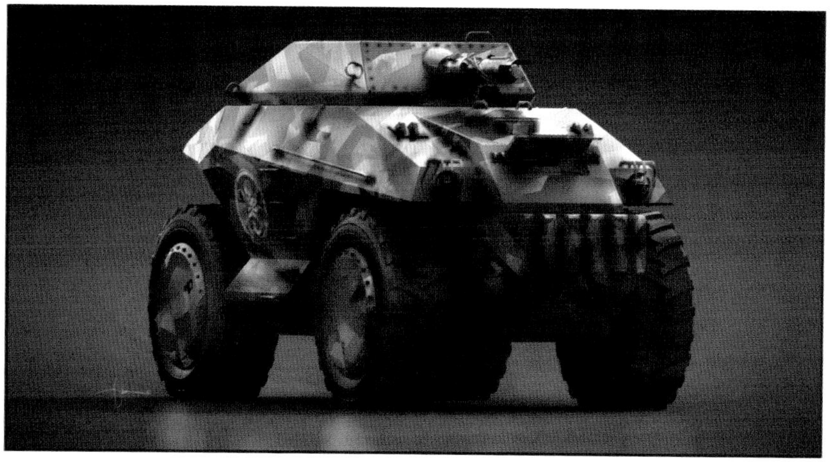

HYDRA MINI TANK

"The Mini Tank came into the script very late," Simon said. "When I got the task to design it, the production in England had already purchased a JCB tractor as the base. So I researched the dimensions and doodled three variations over that package, based on Joe Johnston's briefing. My final illustrations show some color, especially a bold red stripe, suggesting Hydra doesn't bother hiding."

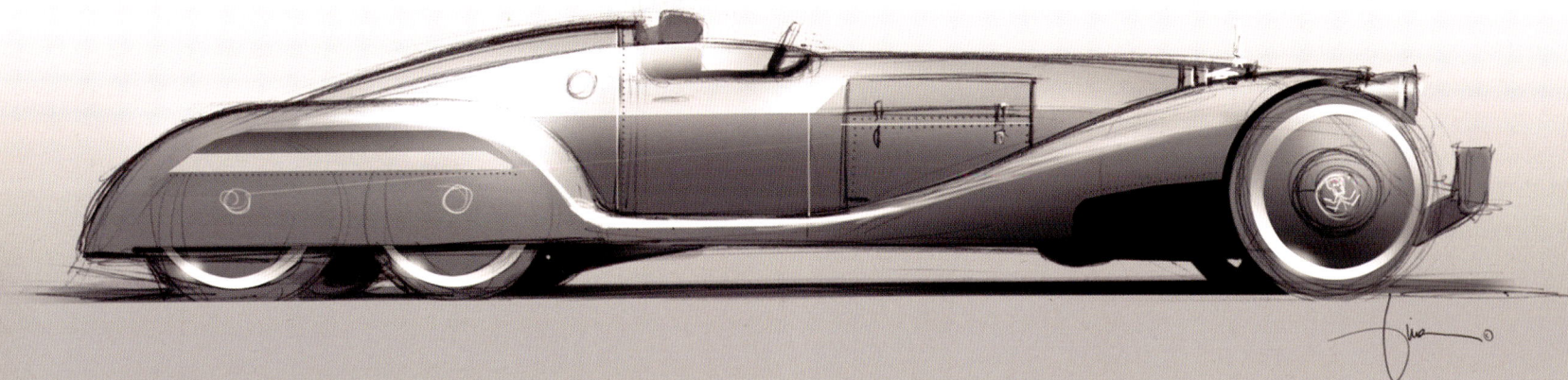

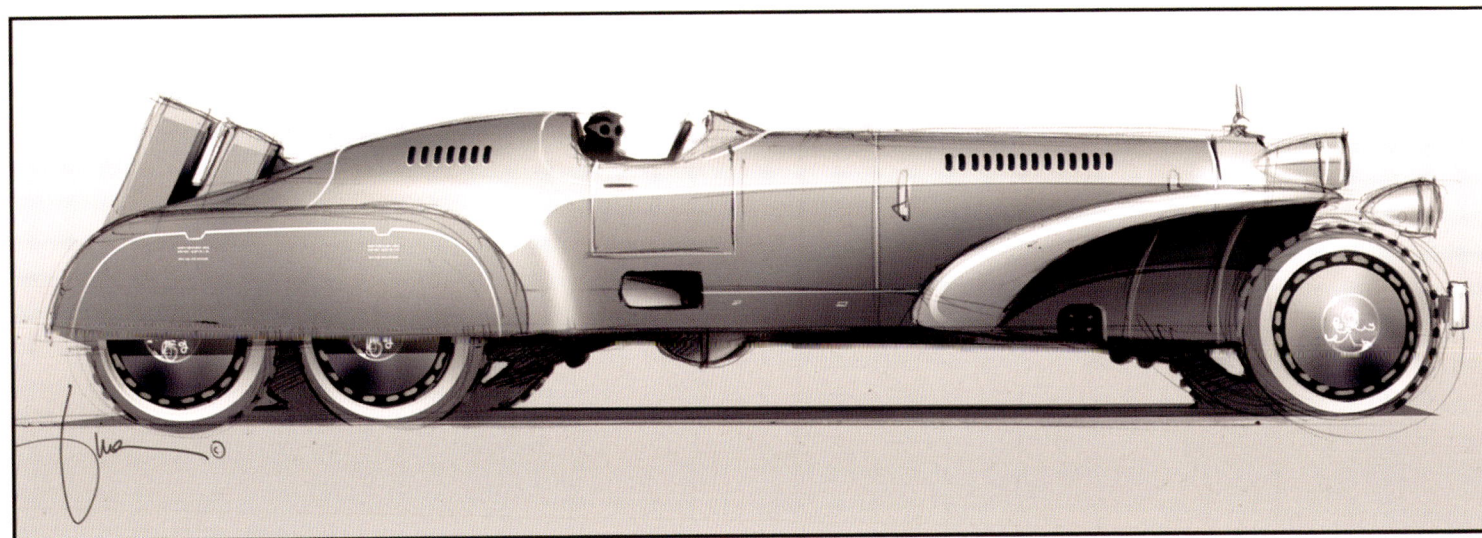

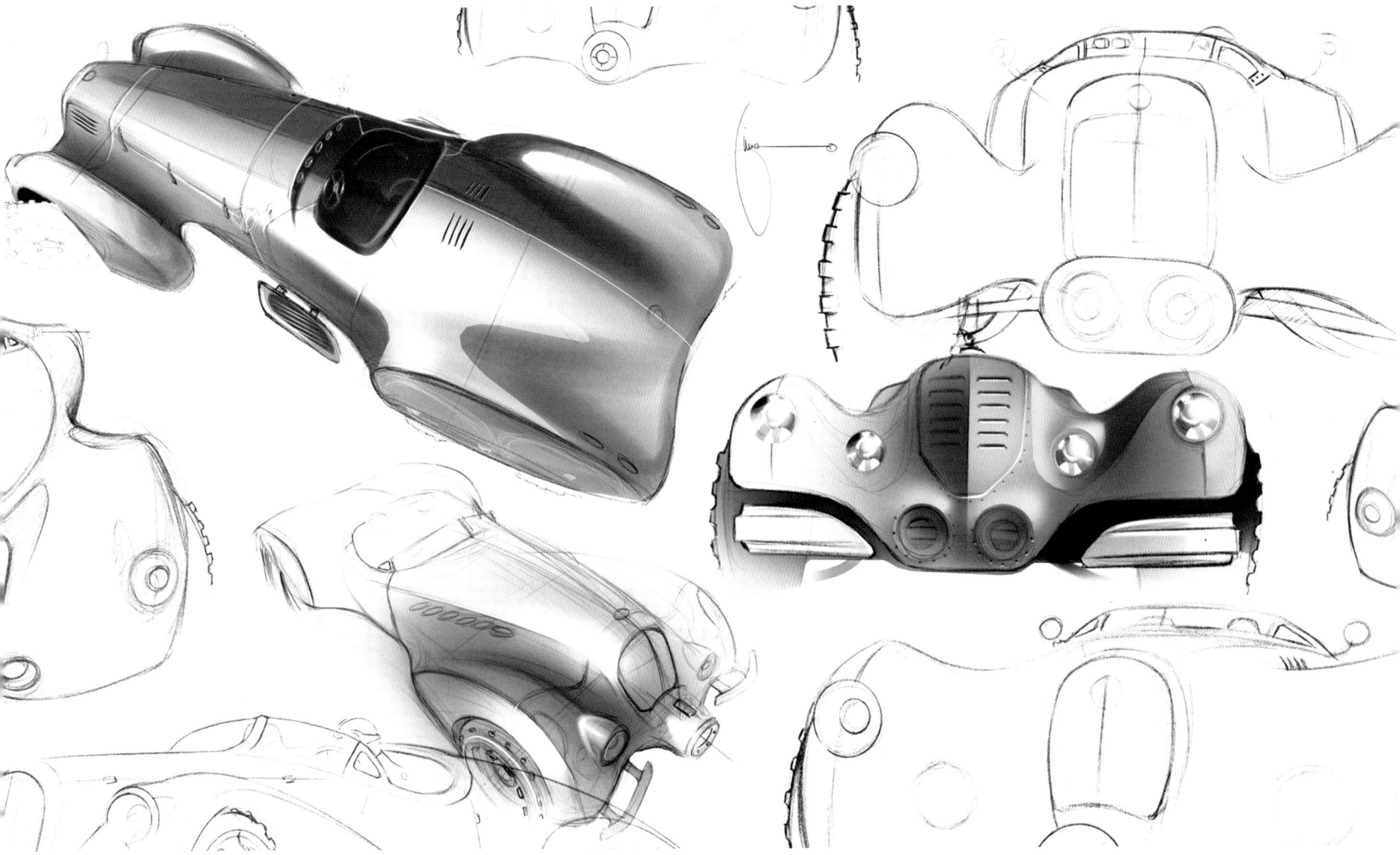

Concept art by Daniel Simon.

SCHMIDT'S COUPE

Said Simon, "In the story, Schmidt's Coupe is supposed to be the fastest car of its time. Not due to its aerodynamics, but its incredible power — a conventional, 16-cylinder supercharged aircraft engine. As a car designer by heart, I was excited and terrified by the task. Joe, Rick and I spent quite some time researching Coupes of the '40s and defining the style of it. In the beginning, I envisioned Schmidt's car shaped like a 1937 Auto Union Type C streamliner, but I soon understood Joe was looking for something classic and upright."

SCHMIDT'S COUPE

"Due to the sheer size of Schmidt's Coupe, we soon decided to use a truck chassis and truck wheels," Simon said. "That also meant I had to spend serious time on finding elegant curves and shapes on that giant scale while maintaining a small, real-size cockpit. If you scale a classic car up to that size, it would look ridiculous. Every bit is designed from scratch to balance the proportions. I spent days to adjust the highlights on the glossy painted rear fenders in 3D software, knowing that my data would go straight to the workshops overseas."

Simon's hard work paid off when he saw the finished result. "I could not be happier with the final production car. Seeing it for the first time in person during filming at Shepperton Studios in London was amazing. Little details like the asymmetric bulb on the engine hood turned out to look very cool in the establishing shot of the car."

Concept art by Daniel Simon.

HYDRA PLANES

The filmmakers' main goal in designing the Hydra
vehicles was to keep them simple and believable, an
aesthetic they also applied to Hydra's many aircraft.

Concept art by Nathan Schroeder, vehicle design by Daniel Simon.

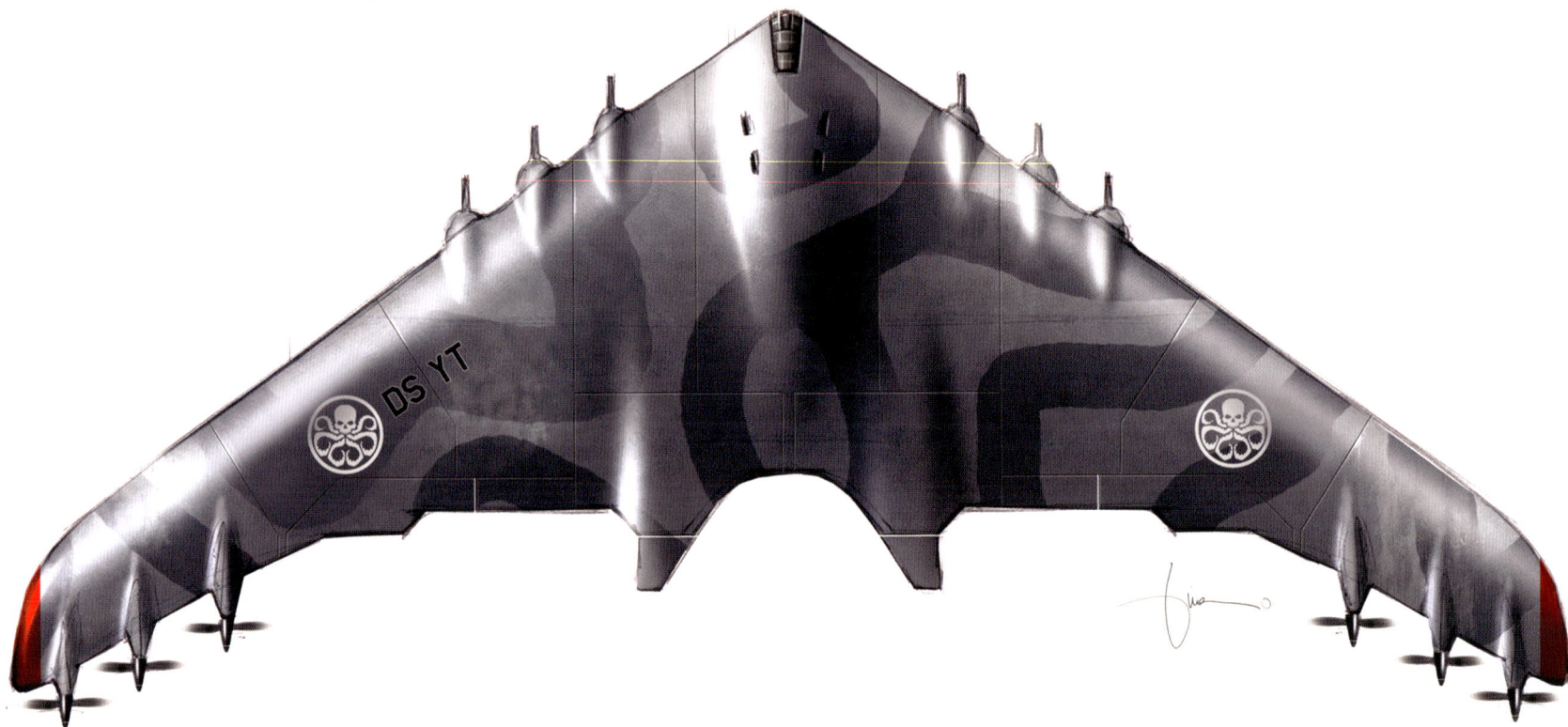

"When I started on the film, some vehicle ideas were already conceptualized by the amazing production designer, Rick Heinrichs," Simon said. "One of those pencil drawings showed an enormous flying wing, with engine pods that are small propeller planes themselves and the wing interiors being as large as a hangar." With Simon's help, this idea slowly took shape as the Hydra Bomber, also known as "Schwarze Witwe."

"The Hydra Bomber is a jet-powered craft with a 540-foot wingspan," Simon said. "The additional eight propellers help liftoff and are not required for cruise. Those propellers actually belong to small bomber planes, using the flying wing as their mother ship. That makes the flying wing actually an aircraft carrier, a weapon system many parties looked into during the 1940s."

Concept art by Daniel Simon.

"The first thing I explored was possible silhouettes, the most visual aspect of a flying wing since the profile is minimal," Simon said. Keeping in mind Johnston's emphasis on simplicity and believability, Simon focused on a clean outline with staggered engines and an organically shaped cockpit area.

The massive Hydra Bomber proved a difficult undertaking, even for a seasoned veteran like Simon. "That vehicle was the toughest to model for me in 3D," Simon said. "The subtleties of aircraft design only alarm you when you actually have to do it. I thought I cracked it when I started pulling the wing tips more and more down, creating a negative V in front view. Flying wings don't photograph well, only in very few views. The trick then was to drag its wingtips down as much as I could, and finally it got a silhouette."

Concept art by Daniel Simon.

185

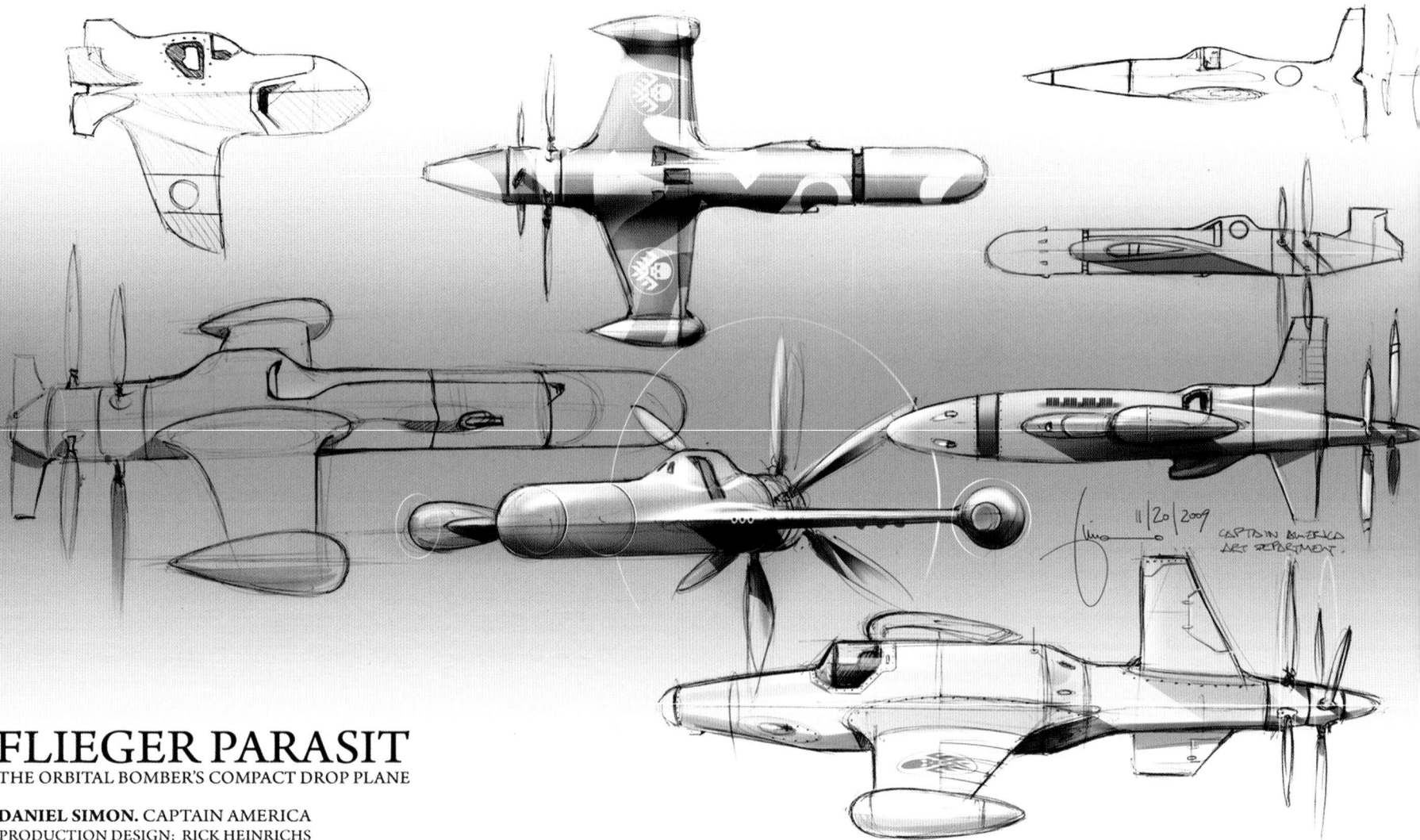

FLIEGER PARASIT
THE ORBITAL BOMBER'S COMPACT DROP PLANE

DANIEL SIMON. CAPTAIN AMERICA
PRODUCTION DESIGN: RICK HEINRICHS

Again taking his cue from Johnston, Simon said he kept the Hydra Drone plane — also known as the "Drehflugler" — as simple as possible, without any "fancy gimmicks and shapes.

Joe kept mentioning 'flying bomb.' So I turned that problem into the solution: The front is literally the bomb. And once released, the plane has a stubby, noseless appearance."

Concept art by Daniel Simon.

186

FLIEGER PARASIT
THE ORBITAL BOMBER'S COMPACT DROP PLANE
DANIEL SIMON. CAPTAIN AMERICA
PRODUCTION DESIGN: RICK HEINRICHS

FLIEGER PARASIT
THE ORBITAL BOMBER'S COMPACT DROP PLANE
DANIEL SIMON. CAPTAIN AMERICA
PRODUCTION DESIGN: RICK HEINRICHS

FLIEGER PARASIT
THE ORBITAL BOMBER'S COMPACT DROP PLANE
DANIEL SIMON. CAPTAIN AMERICA
PRODUCTION DESIGN: RICK HEINRICHS

Concept art by Nathan Schroeder.

Concept art by Mauro Borelli.

Experimental German propulsion systems of the 1940s —
particularly that of the Focke-Wulf Triebflugel, which was
capable of vertical take-off and landing — directly impacted the

Hydra Drone's final design. With the Triebflugel sitting on its tail in
the vertical position, its rotors functioned in a manner similar to
those of a helicopter; in flight, they acted like a massive propeller.

Concept art by Nathan Schroeder.

Concept art by
Daniel Simon.

VIELE GRÜSSE NACH NEW YORK!

"The most simple and obvious solution appears sometimes only after endless explorations," Simon said. "The final design of the Hydra Drone Plane had the realistic and menacing simplicity Joe was looking for."

HYDRA MOTORCYCLE

"The Hydra Bikes are a classic example of movie design," Simon said. "I worked the most time on them of all the Hydra vehicles, though what you see in the final film is a quick sketch from my very last day on the show. Filmmaking is an organic process. Things change every day, which is a great challenge."

The way vehicles are crafted for film has changed dramatically through the years, now relying heavily on 3D computer programs. "Proportions on vehicles are extremely sensitive, so I always start very early to juggle volumes in 3D," Simon said. "That allows the director to look at it from all angles, and it helps me to adjust the position of the rider — a crucial deal on a bike."

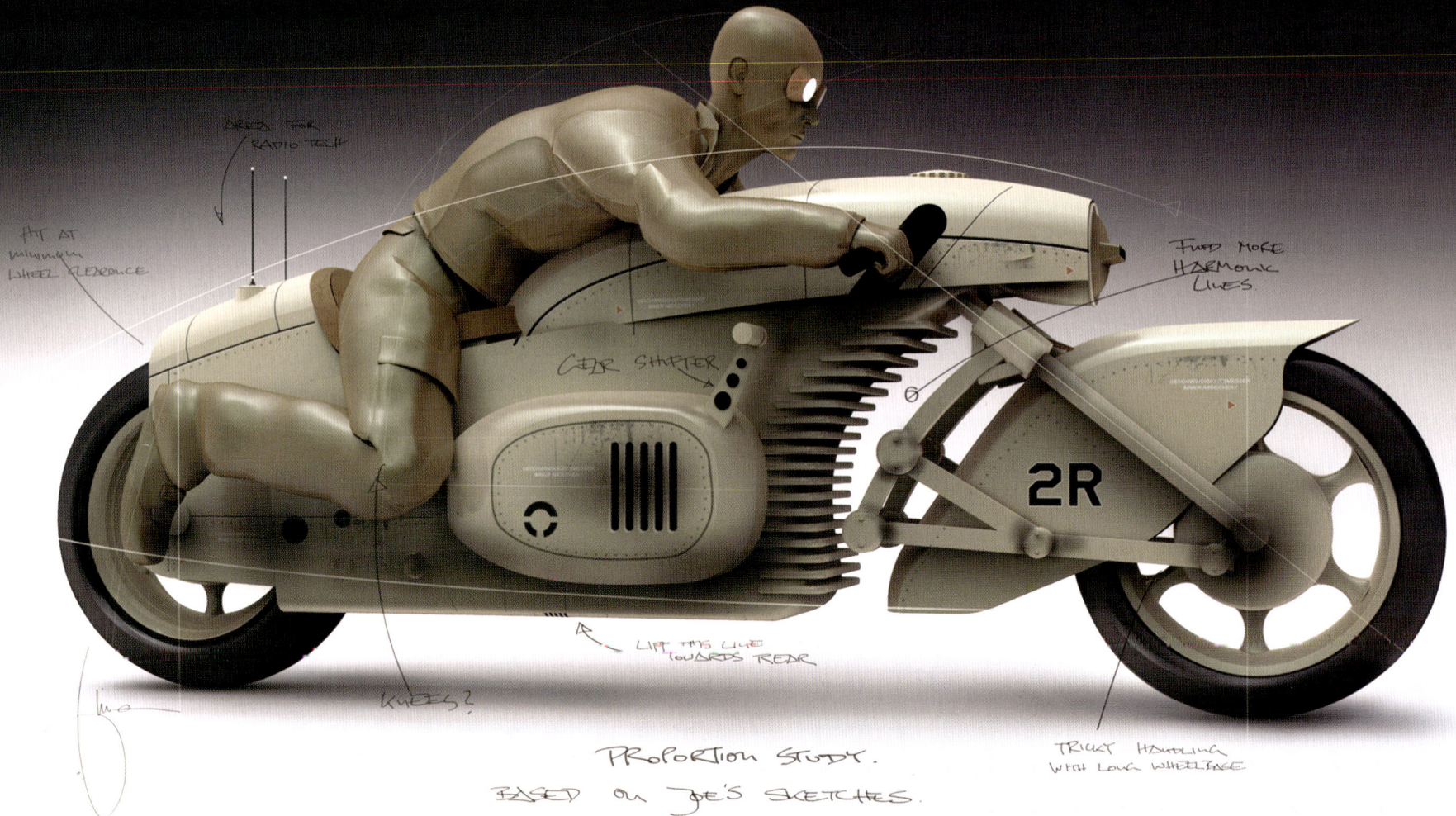

2R

PROPORTION STUDY.
BASED ON JOE'S SKETCHES.

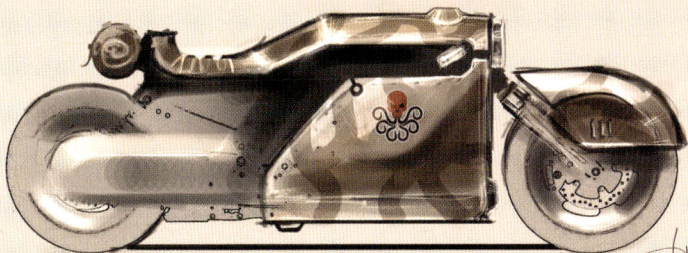

HYDRA BIKE
VROOOM.

DANIEL SIMON. CAPTAIN AMERICA ART DEPARTMENT 2010
PRODUCTION DESIGN: RICK HEINRICHS

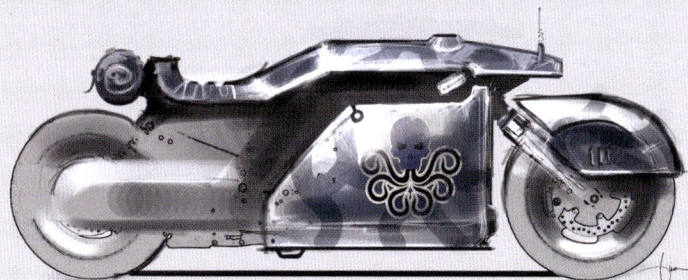

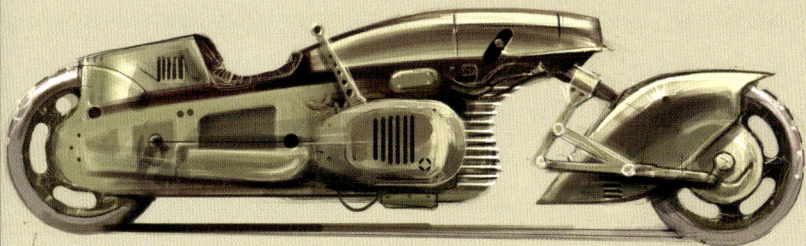

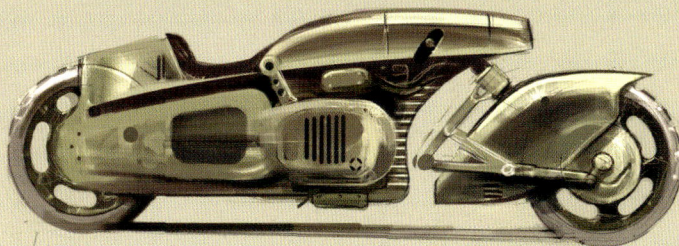

HYDRA BIKE
VROOOM.

DANIEL SIMON. CAPTAIN AMERICA ART DEPARTMENT 2010
PRODUCTION DESIGN: RICK HEINRICHS

HYDRA BIKE
IDEATION PHASE

DANIEL SIMON. CAPTAIN AMERICA ART DEPARTMENT 2010
PRODUCTION DESIGN: RICK HEINRICHS

HYDRA BIKE
IDEATION PHASE

DANIEL SIMON. CAPTAIN AMERICA ART DEPARTMENT 2010
PRODUCTION DESIGN: RICK HEINRICHS

Concept art by Daniel Simon.

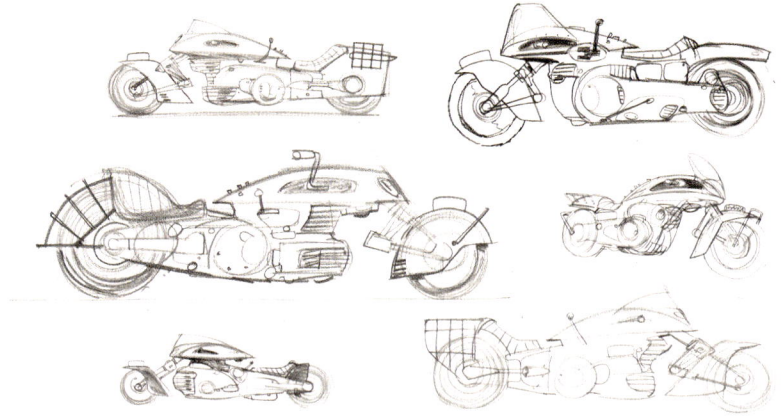

Early Hydra motorcycle sketches by Director Joe Johnston.

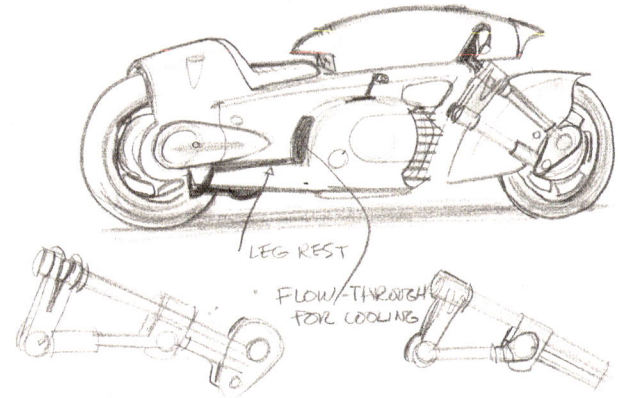

LEG REST

FLOW-THROUGH FOR COOLING

HYDRA BIKE
FINAL STAGE. OVERLAY OVER PRODUCTION CHASSIS

DANIEL SIMON. CAPTAIN AMERICA ART DEPARTMENT 2010
PRODUCTION DESIGN: RICK HEINRICHS

STEP 20

HYDRA BIKE
FINAL STAGE. OVERLAY OVER PRODUCTION CHASSIS

DANIEL SIMON. CAPTAIN AMERICA ART DEPARTMENT 2010
PRODUCTION DESIGN: RICK HEINRICHS

HYDRA BIKE
FINAL STAGE. OVERLAY OVER PRODUCTION CHASSIS

DANIEL SIMON. CAPTAIN AMERICA ART DEPARTMENT 2010
PRODUCTION DESIGN: RICK HEINRICHS

Concept art by Daniel Simon.

DS 0912

"We worked for the longest time with a stretched Harley-Davidson chassis, and I carefully translated Joe's visions of a long wheelbase onto that package," Simon said. "With the filming schedule coming closer, the production decided for an Enduro-Offroad bike as the base — the most opposite of a Harley. The script asked for actions that would have been difficult for stuntmen to perform on a long bike. So I translated our long wheelbase design onto the purchased Enduro bike, which led to the final design."

Johnston also added grenades and two tank-mounted guns; a windshield was incorporated to help conceal the modern donor bike. As the script developed, the story called for a greater number of Hydra Bikes — necessitating a simpler design, but one still capable of covering most of the underlying bike, so they could be manufactured on schedule in high numbers for shooting.

Concept art by Andy Park.

Concept art by Daniel Simon.

HYDRA SUBMARINE

The Hydra Submarine, also known in the film as the "Fieser Dorsch," allowed Simon more creative freedom. "Submarines come in myriad shapes and layouts," Simon said. "In my initial sketches, I tried to play with as many as I could, also offering awkward concepts that could work both below and above water: counter-rotating props mid-ship, big wing shapes, outriggers, multiple engines."

Concept art by Daniel Simon.

D. SIMON . MARVEL ART DEPARTMENT 2010

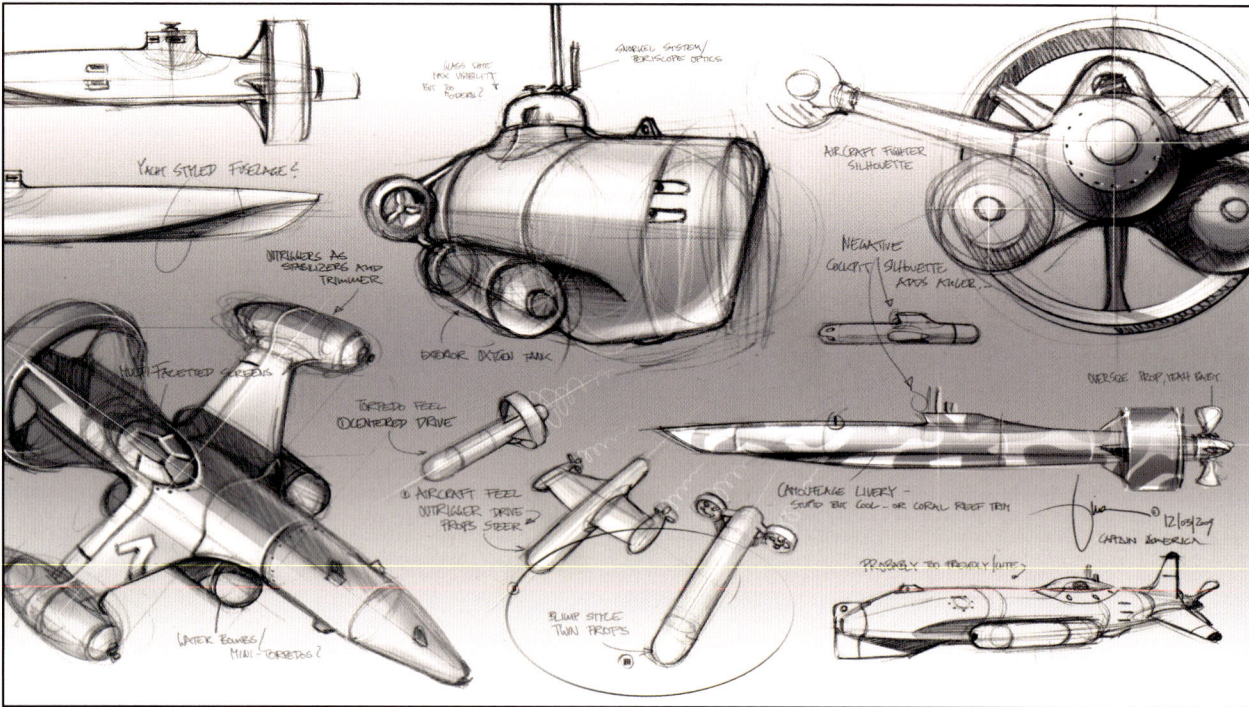

YACHT STYLED FUSELAGE?

OUTRIGGERS AS STABILIZERS AND TRIMMER

HIGH FACETTED SCREENS

WATER BOMBS / MINI-TORPEDOS?

GLASS DOME MAX VISIBILITY FOR 3D FODDER?

GIMBAL SYSTEM / PERISCOPE OPTICS

EXTERIOR OXYGEN TANK

TORPEDO FEEL OFF-CENTERED DRIVE

AIRCRAFT FEEL OUTRIGGER DRIVE PROPS STEER

BLIMP STYLE TWIN PROPS

AIRCRAFT FIGHTER SILHOUETTE

NEGATIVE COCKPIT SILHOUETTE ADDS ANGER

OVERSIZE PROP, YEAH BABY

CAMOUFLAGE LIVERY - STEALTH BUT COOL - OR CORAL REEF TRIM

PROBABLY TOO FRIENDLY / CUTE?

CAPTAIN AMERICA 12/03/2019

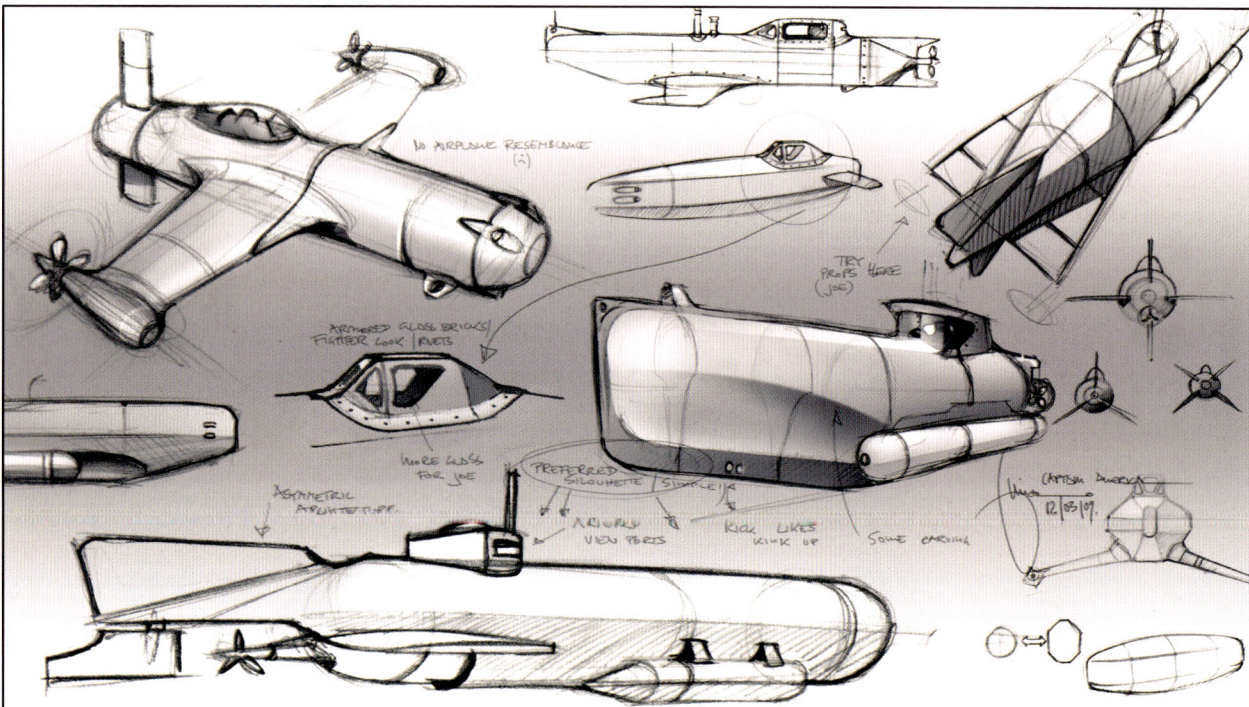

1/2 AIRPLANE RESEMBLANCE (?)

ARMORED GLASS BRICKS / FIGHTER LOOK / RIVETS

MORE GLASS FOR JOE

ASYMMETRIC ARCHITECTURE.

ARMORED VIEW PORTS

TRY PROPS HERE (JOE)

PREFERRED SILHOUETTE (SIMPLE!?)

JOE LIKES KINK UP

SOME CARVING

CAPTAIN AMERICA 12/03/19.

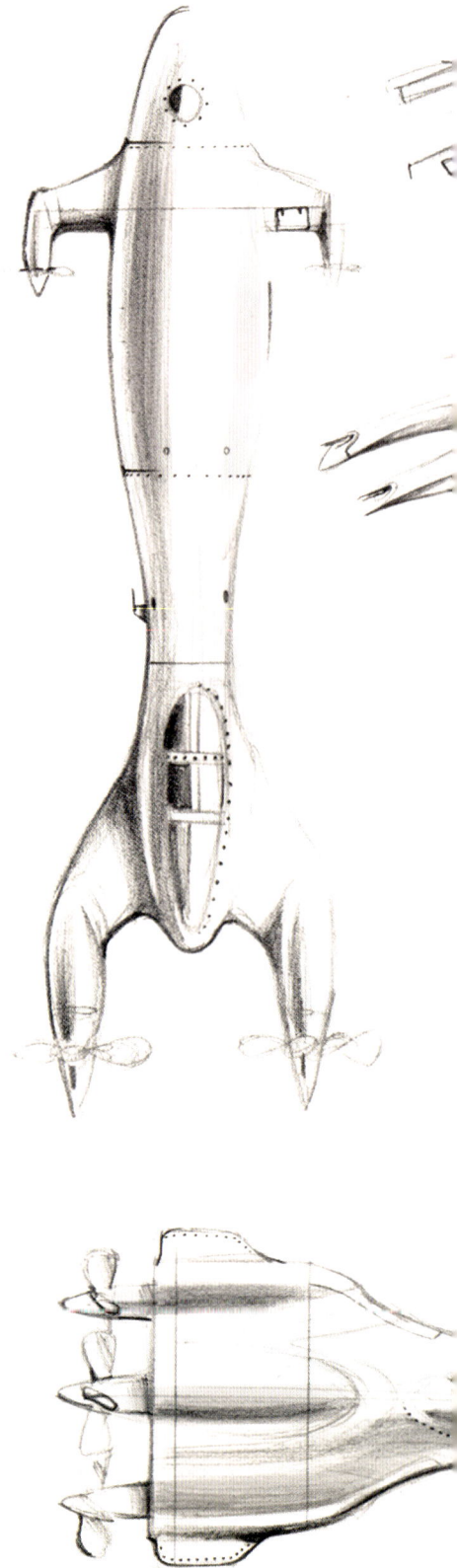

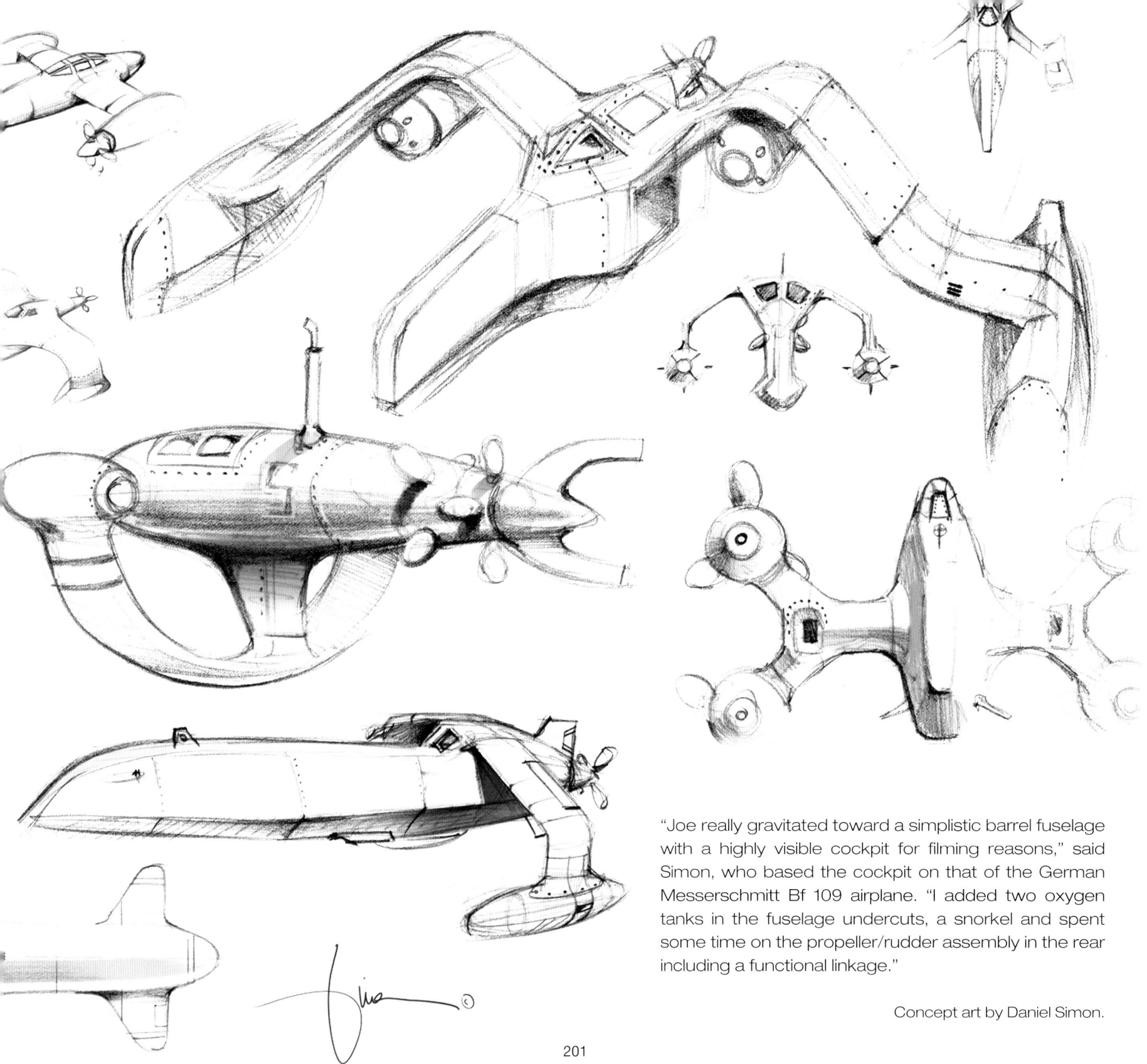

"Joe really gravitated toward a simplistic barrel fuselage with a highly visible cockpit for filming reasons," said Simon, who based the cockpit on that of the German Messerschmitt Bf 109 airplane. "I added two oxygen tanks in the fuselage undercuts, a snorkel and spent some time on the propeller/rudder assembly in the rear including a functional linkage."

Concept art by Daniel Simon.

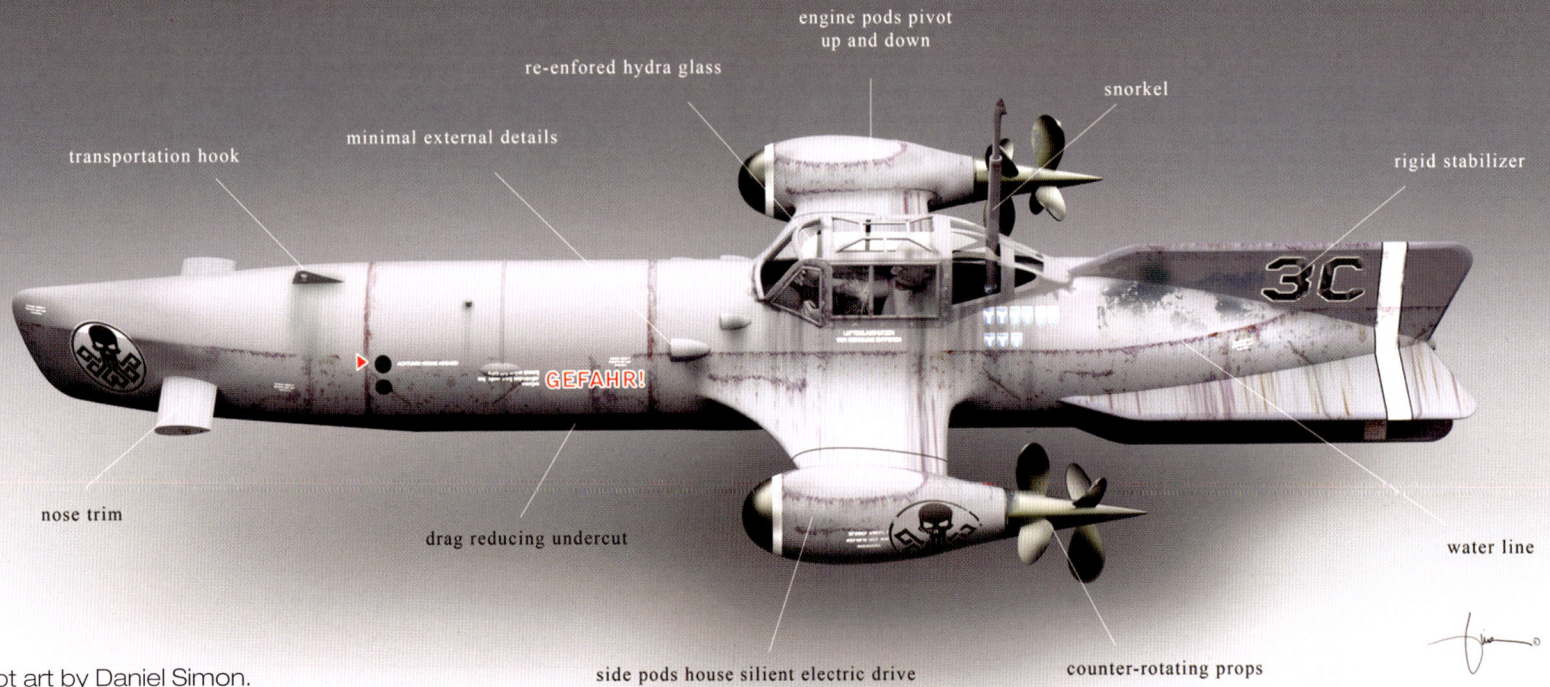

engine pods pivot
up and down

re-enfored hydra glass

snorkel

minimal external details

rigid stabilizer

transportation hook

nose trim

GEFAHR!

3C

drag reducing undercut

water line

side pods house silient electric drive

counter-rotating props

Concept art by Daniel Simon.

"The position of the propellers was of interest for the story," Simon said. "Captain America would dive after the submersing boat — so either the propellers would add some cool underwater action, or be in the way. I soon offered the alternative of two propeller pods on outriggers, which would also render rudders obsolete."

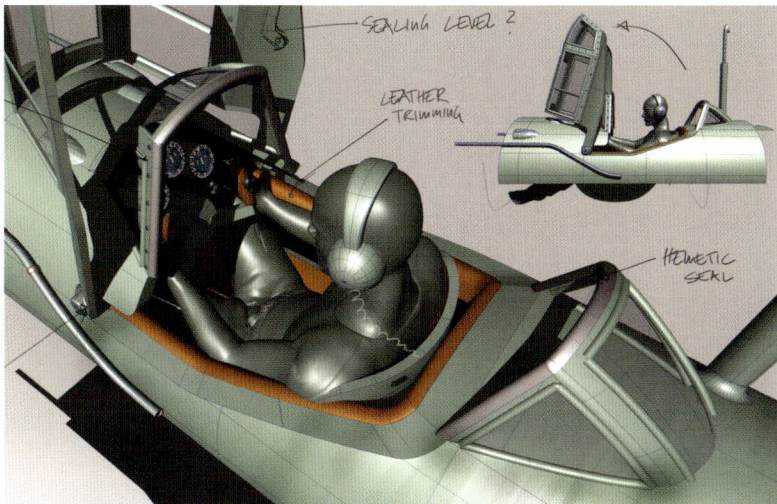

SEALING LEVEL ?

LEATHER TRIMMING

HELMETIC SEAL

VERTICAL / HORIZONTAL
RUDDER

ELECTRIC ENGINE
NACELLE

BALLISTIC TWIN TANK

SNORKEL

COCKPIT HATCH

Concept art by Daniel Simon.

NOSE TRIM

GEFAHR!

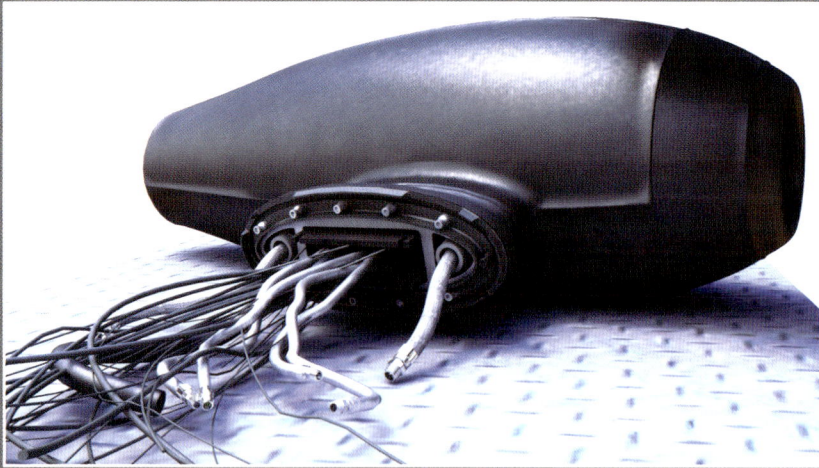
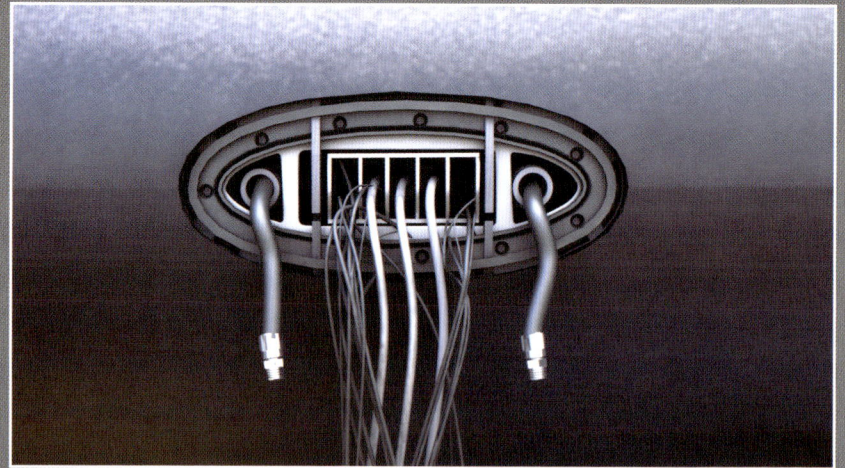
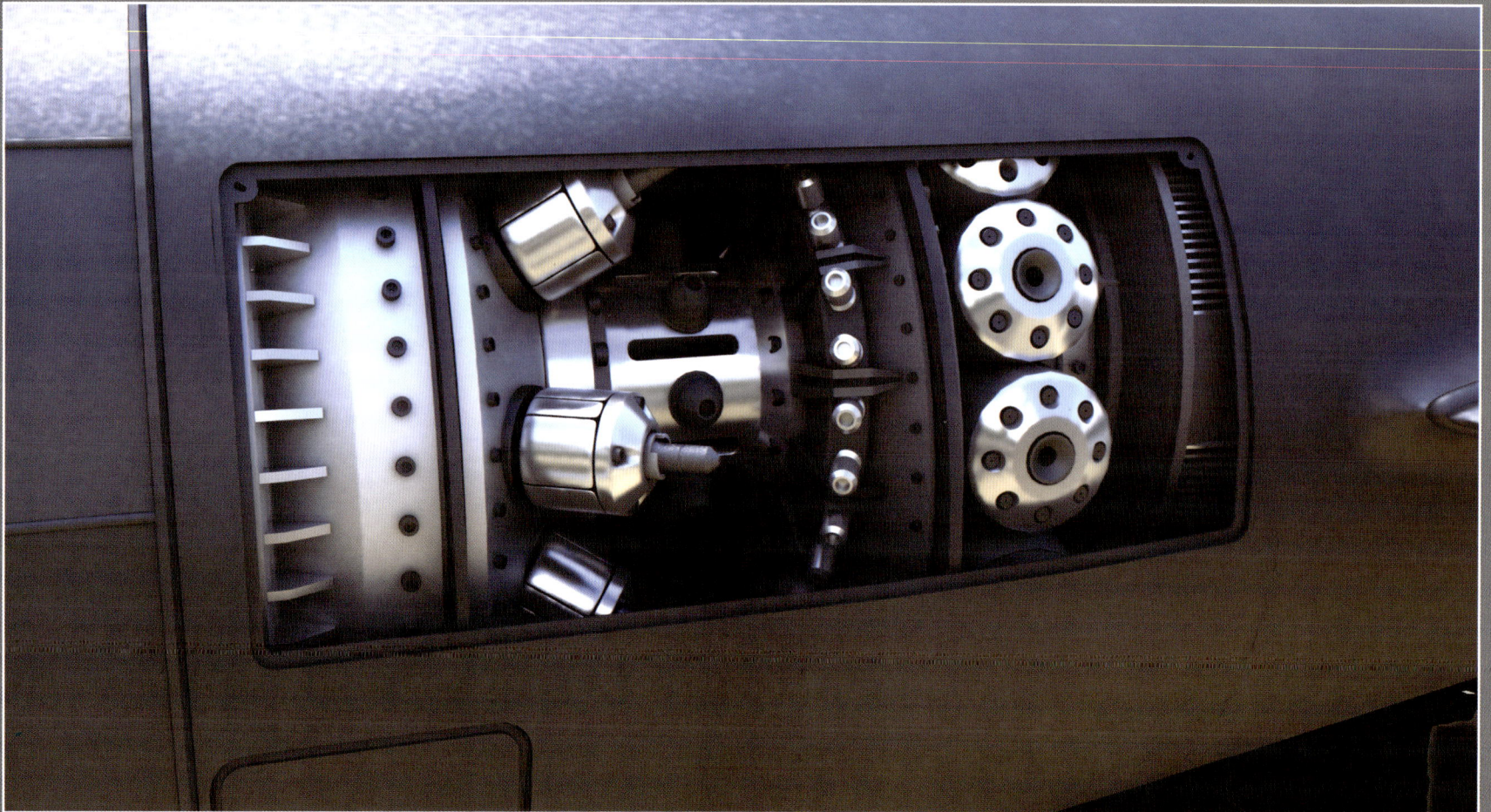

The Hydra Submarine's layout proved popular with filmmakers, as it allowed some propeller action to be seen in close-up shots of the pilot. In pursuit of more advanced Hydra technology, the propellers were replaced with water jets. The canopy was also streamlined in the final design.

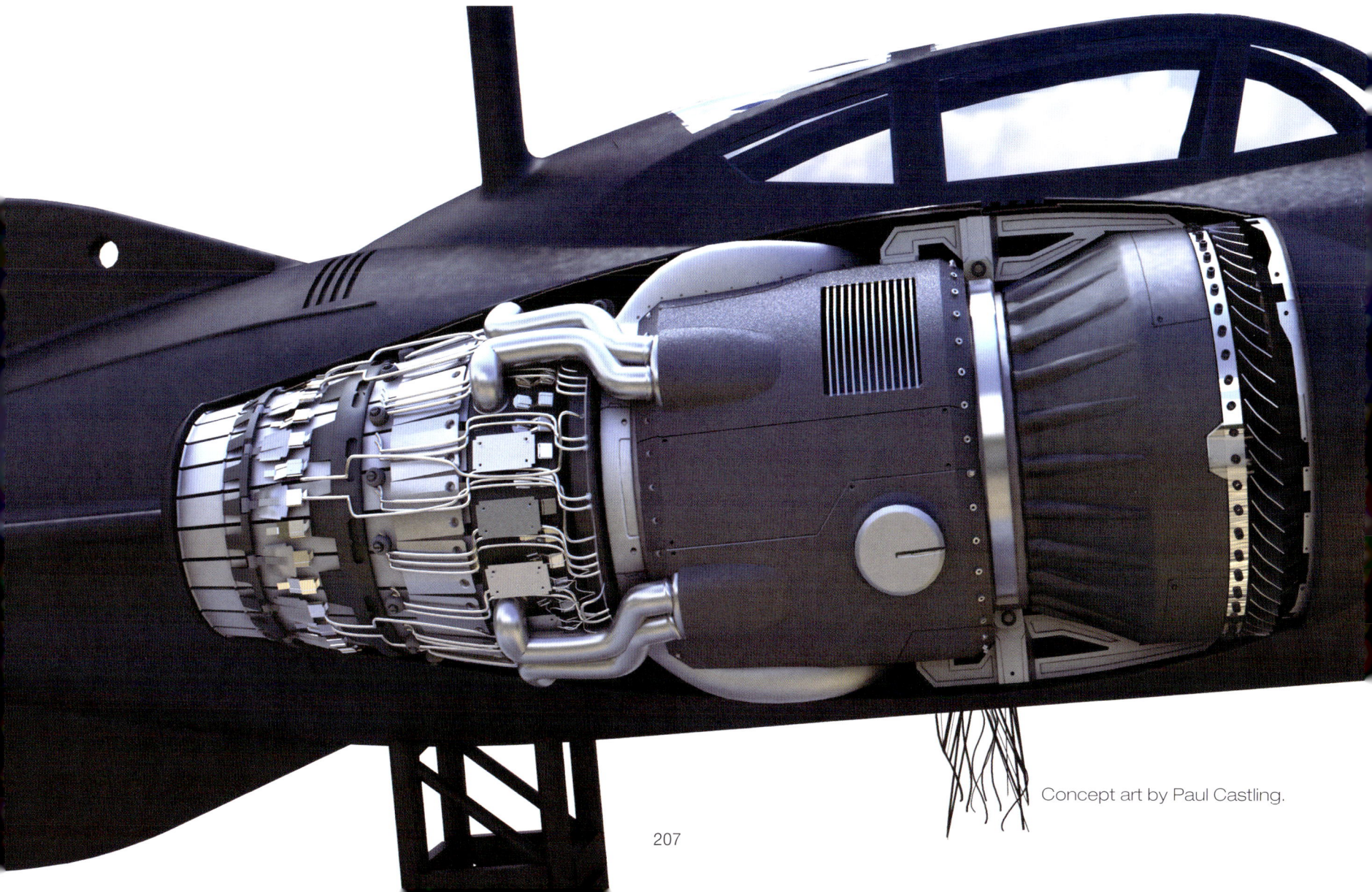

Concept art by Paul Castling.

With all the design elements in place, the sleek and silent Hydra Submarine became what would have been a technological marvel for the 1940s — with water jets allowing for steering, a front rudder and internal systems trimming the boat, and special Hydra glass offering better visibility.

Concept art by Henrick Tamm.

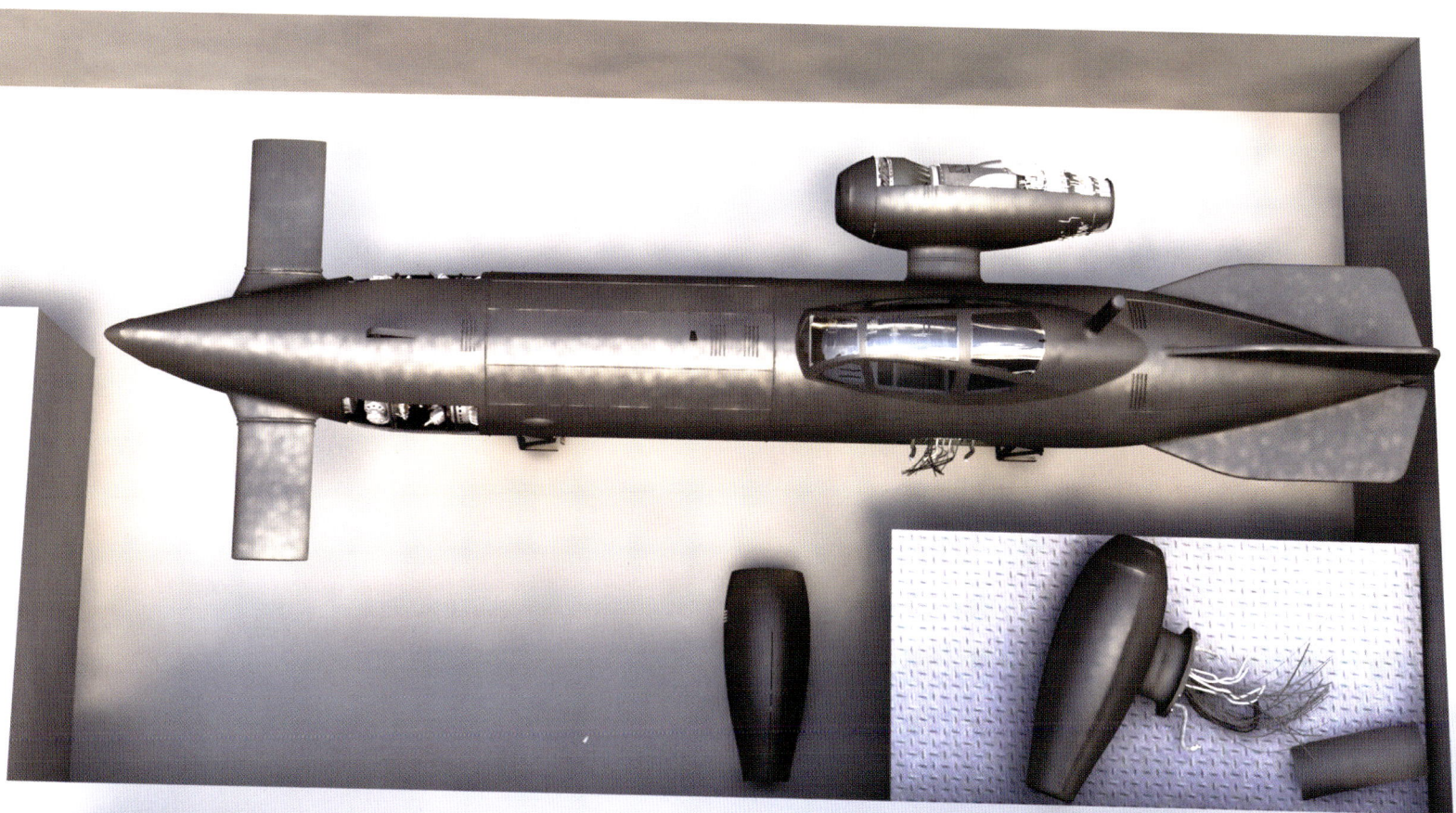

Concept art by Paul Castling.

Concept art by
Paul Castling.

Production still.

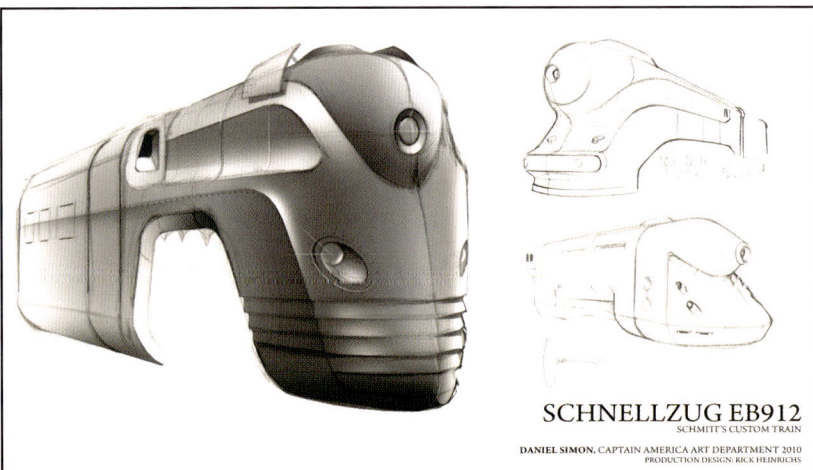

SCHNELLZUG EB912
SCHMITT'S CUSTOM TRAIN

DANIEL SIMON. CAPTAIN AMERICA ART DEPARTMENT 2010
PRODUCTION DESIGN: RICK HEINRICHS

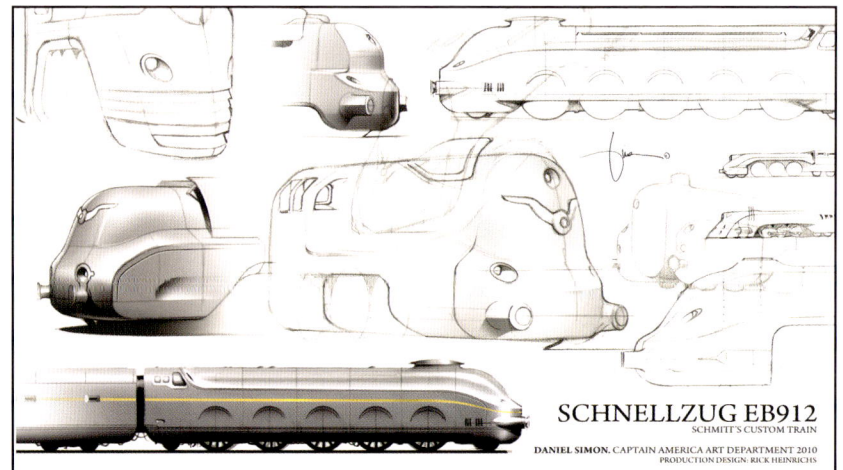

SCHNELLZUG EB912
SCHMITT'S CUSTOM TRAIN

DANIEL SIMON. CAPTAIN AMERICA ART DEPARTMENT 2010
PRODUCTION DESIGN: RICK HEINRICHS

HYDRA TRAINS

SCHNELLZUG EB912
SCHMIDT'S CUSTOM TRAIN
DANIEL SIMON CAPTAIN AMERICA ART DEPARTMENT 2010
PROFILE TOP DESIGN. RICK HEINRICHS

When it came to the Hydra Train, Simon felt more pressure on the job than he usually does. "My father collects steam-train models, hundreds of them, and knows quite a bit about it," Simon said. "So I wanted to get the train right."

SCHNELLZUG EB912
SCHMIDT'S CUSTOM TRAIN
DANIEL SIMON CAPTAIN AMERICA ART DEPARTMENT 2010
PRODUCTION DESIGN. RICK HEINRICHS

Concept art by Daniel Simon.

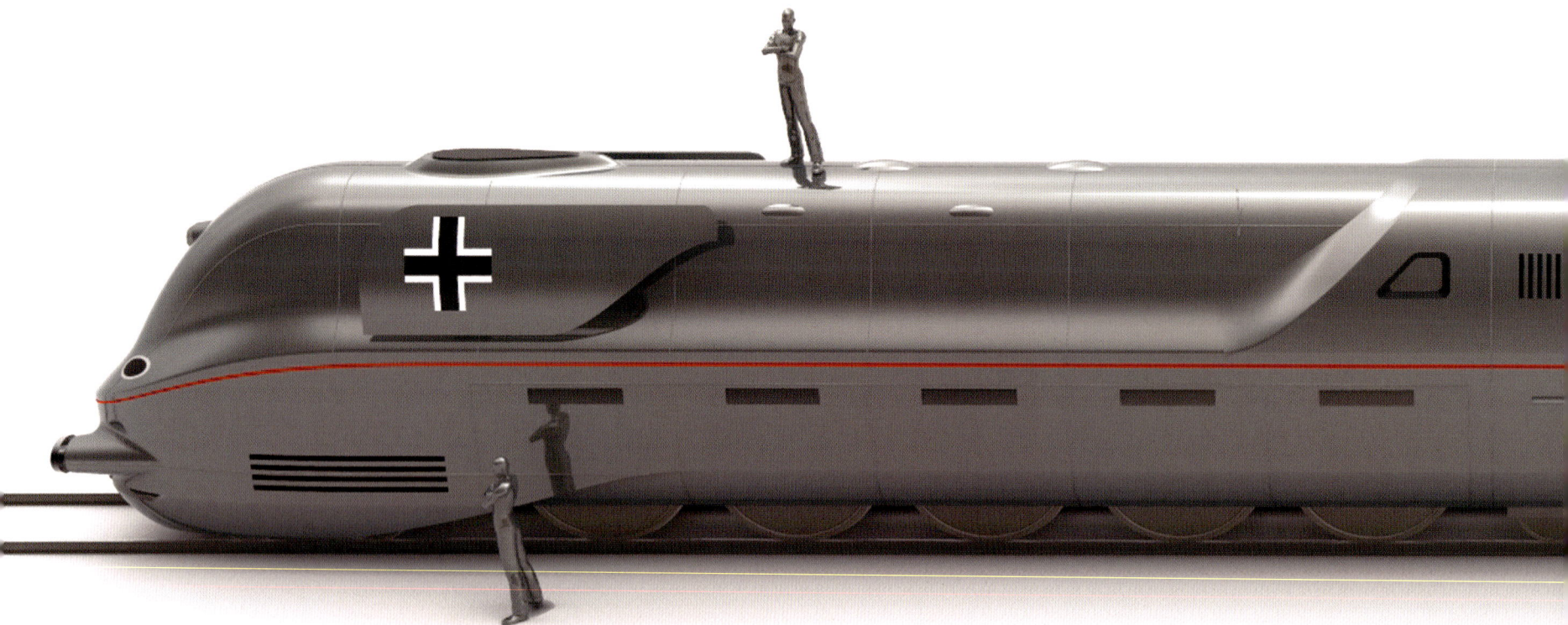

"The '30s were a vast style reference," Simon said. "Steam trains all over the world fashioned gorgeous streamlined body panels. It was the wonderful time of art deco. My first sketches tried to echo those looks without copying it. Our Hydra Train is not only authentic with its streamlined look, but also innovative in a Hydra sense with its tandem layout."

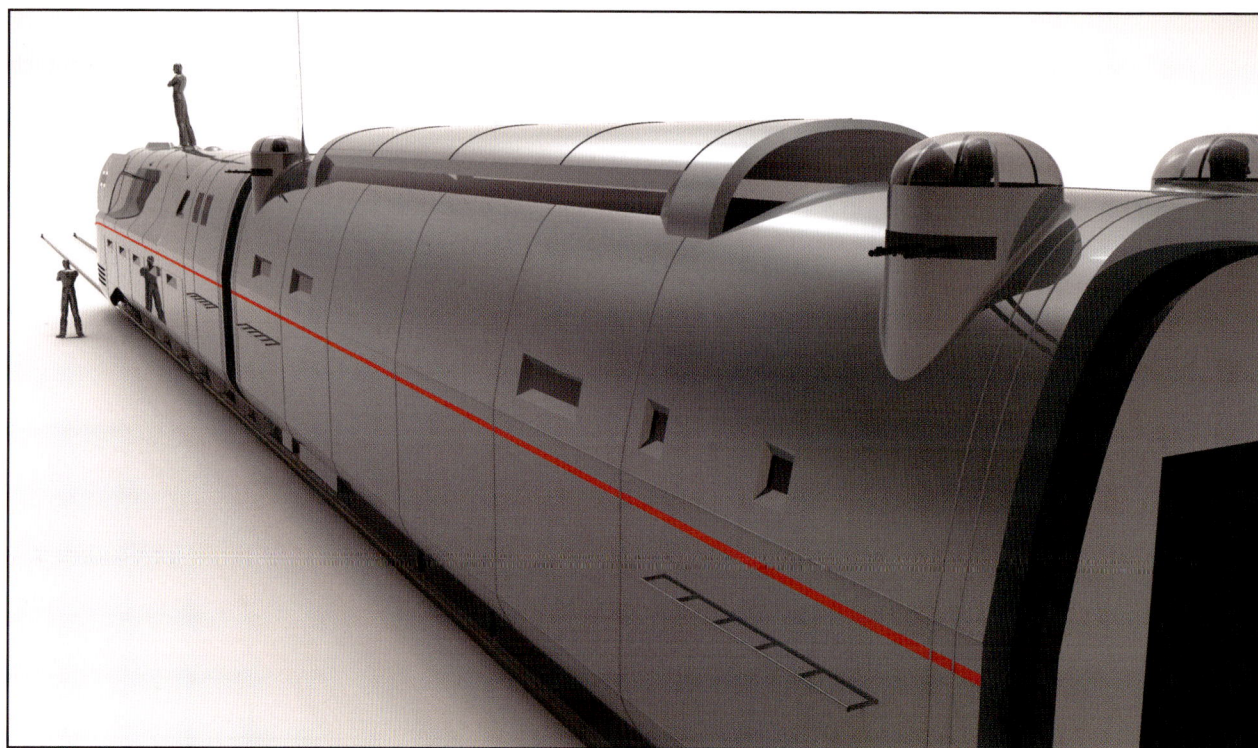

Concept art by Daniel Simon.

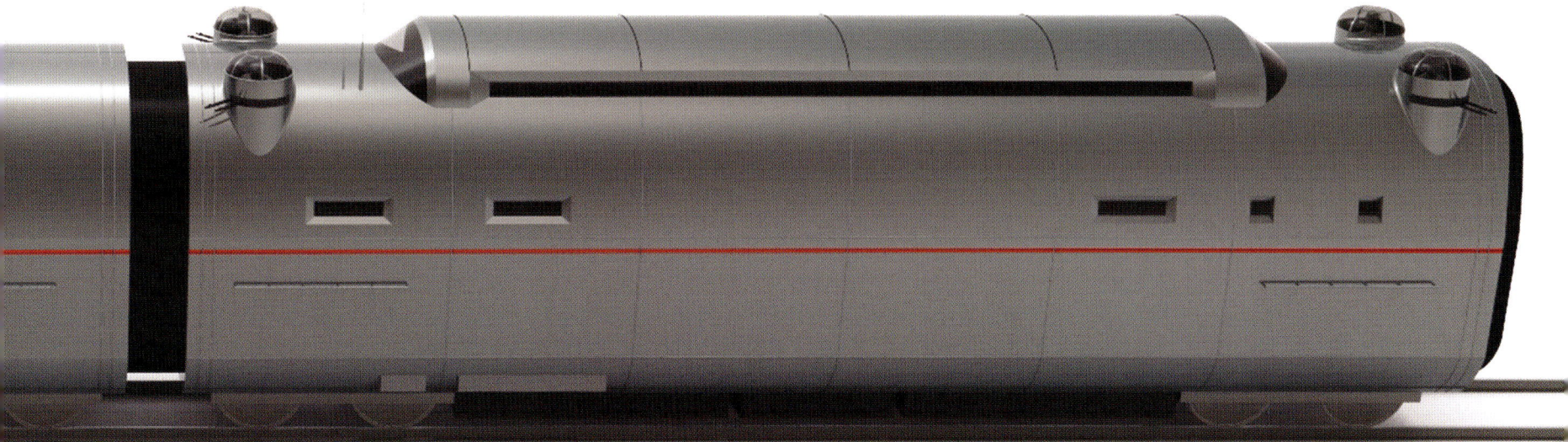

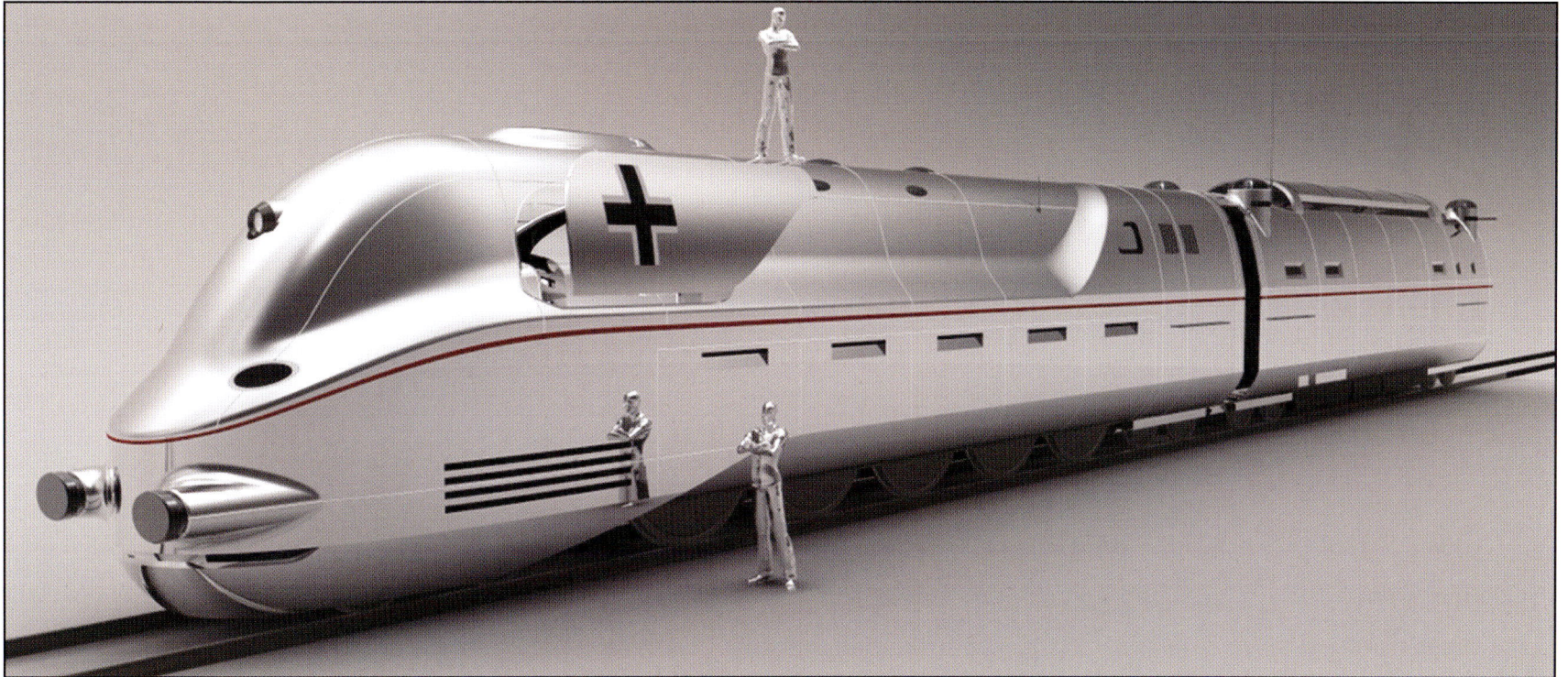

CHAPTER SIX

SEEING ACTION

Amazing action sequences are at the center of every Marvel Studios film. Great characters and stories keep viewers interested, but stunning effects and exciting fights are what have fans cheering in the aisles. And as any action-movie aficionado will tell you, there's nothing more fun than a classic car chase.

For Director Joe Johnston to efficiently orchestrate an elaborate sequence like the pivotal Kruger Chase Scene in *Captain America: The First Avenger*, storyboards are used to pace and plot out the action. These single-panel drawings, resembling comic-book illustrations when placed side-by-side, help determine the best angles from which to shoot a scene and are the first step in translating a film's script into a visual medium. Due to today's ever-evolving technology, finished storyboards are often animated in a rudimentary fashion, creating an animatic. Invaluable to the crew, animatics not only dictate a particular scene's action, but also provide everyone on set with a unified idea of what each sequence will entail.

Keyframe art by James Hegedus.

KRUGER CHASE SCENE

When Operation Rebirth — the program responsible for transforming Steve Rogers from a frail weakling into an idealized human specimen — erupts into violence due to the actions of German spy Heinz Kruger, Rogers and Peggy Carter are quick to respond. Rogers' new body is put to the test as he takes off on foot after Kruger's taxi.

SHOT 38

SHOT 41

STEVE LOSES CONTROL OF
HI'S NEW RUNNING ABILITIES

(19)

POLLY W/STEVE
AS HE PASSES BY
CAM. OUT OF CONTROL

ONE SHOT

Ⓐ ➞ ➞Ⓑ
➞Ⓒ

ALLEY OUT

TAXI OUT

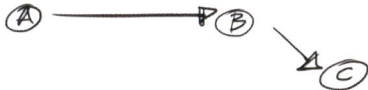

POLLY W/ PAN
FROM OUT OF ALLEYWAY
TOWARDS WINDOW

These storyboards, by Rodolfo Damaggio, not only give the director and cameramen an indication of how the scene should be shot, but even can influence the actors through the facial expressions and body language they depict. Though often overlooked in the grand scheme of filmmaking, the storyboard is an invaluable asset to the crew and a firm visual foundation on which a movie is built.

217

SHOT 56

Old Driver

KRUGER CUTS
OFF INTERSECTION

DRIVER SWERVES
INTO STREET

SHOT 59

TRUCK

SHOT 57

SHOT 60

POV
IN

SHOT 58

Ⓐ

SHOT 61

THUMP!!

STEVE ALMOST
SLIDES OFF

Ⓑ
STEVE
OUT

SHOT 62

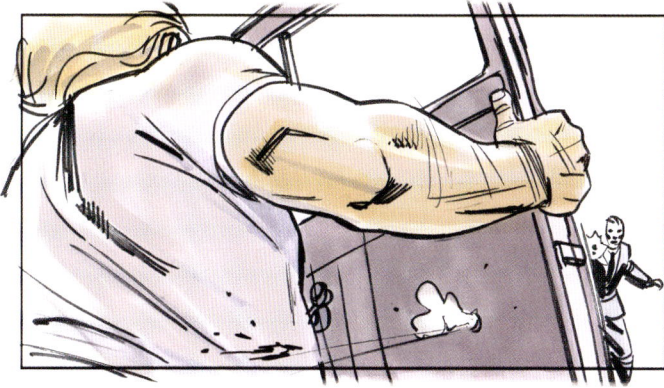

As the chase scene escalates, Rogers catches up to the Hydra spy, proving the strength of his enhanced body in the process. And as Kruger begins to open fire on the soon-to-be hero, viewers are treated to their first glimpse of Captain America's shield — in this case, a taxicab door.

His escape seemingly hopeless, Kruger proves he has one last ace in the hole — in the form of the Hydra Submarine, also called the "Fieser Dorsch." Created by Lead Vehicle Designer Daniel Simon, the sub carries the action to a new location and gives the fight even more of a creative edge.

When the dust settles, Rogers has apprehended his opponent — but Kruger proves just how deadly a threat Hydra is by biting down on a cyanide capsule. So although Steve Rogers' first adventure is for all intents and purposes a success, the threat of Hydra still looms somewhere unknown on the horizon.

CHAPTER SEVEN

THE ART OF WAR

During its brief tenure as an independent production studio, Marvel already has proven on more than one occasion it knows how to make a blockbuster film. But to attract an audience to the theaters in the first place, each Marvel movie must have an equally creative marketing campaign. Luckily for the filmmakers at Marvel Studios, having a background in the world of comic books puts them ahead of the game.

One of the most important aspects of any successful film-marketing campaign is the creation of theatrical and teaser posters. Often the audience's introduction to a film's title character, these one-sheets establish the look and feel of each movie — sometimes with only the bare minimum of information. It's a concept that's not so different from something else Marvel does well: crafting comic-book covers.

N G E

Said Marvel Studios President and *Captain America: The First Avenger* Producer Kevin Feige, "Comic-book covers are meant to catch the eye amidst a rack full of comic-book images. You want one that's going to attract attention. A lot of movie posters are put into theater lobbies, so you need something that stands out. And sometimes, that is done in a poster that is full of dynamic images. And sometimes, that's done with simplicity."

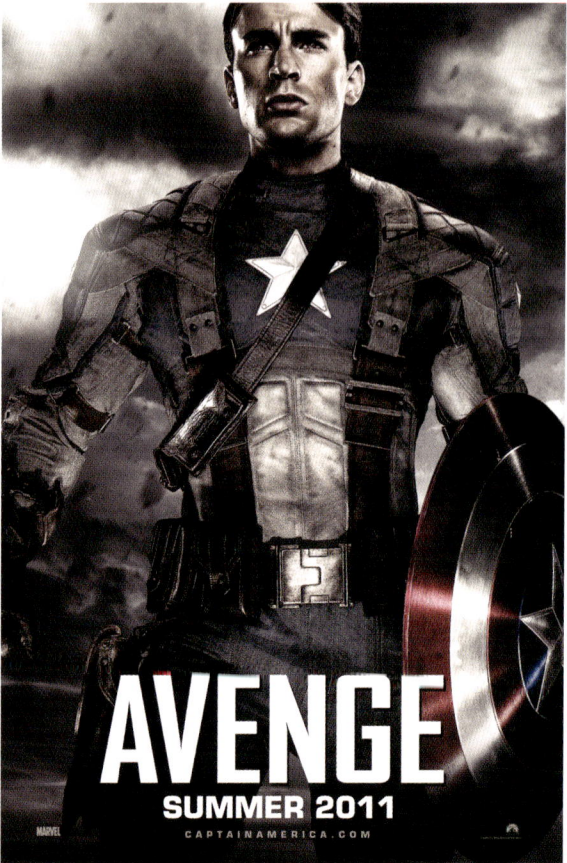

AVENGE
SUMMER 2011
CAPTAINAMERICA.COM

AVENGE

7.22.11
CAPTAINAMERICA.COM

Said Feige, "Every movie campaign starts with us going through dozens and dozens — if not hundreds — of comic-book covers, sending them to the marketing department and the studio to give them a notion and an idea of graphic representation of the characters."

"I would say that we're not mimicking any comic-book cover in particular," Feige said. "But the same type of thought that goes into a comic-book cover to attract attention and get eyeballs goes into the creation of the comic spots." Feige did admit the *Captain America* teaser poster may owe a bit more than most to the efforts of Marvel's print division. "The Captain America pose on the teaser poster you will recognize as an interpretation of a very famous more recent *Captain America* cover."

The marketing campaign for *Captain America: The First Avenger* consisted of much more than a series of posters. From footage shown at San Diego Comic-Con to a TV spot during the Super Bowl, Marvel Studios made sure their company's original icon was back in the spotlight.

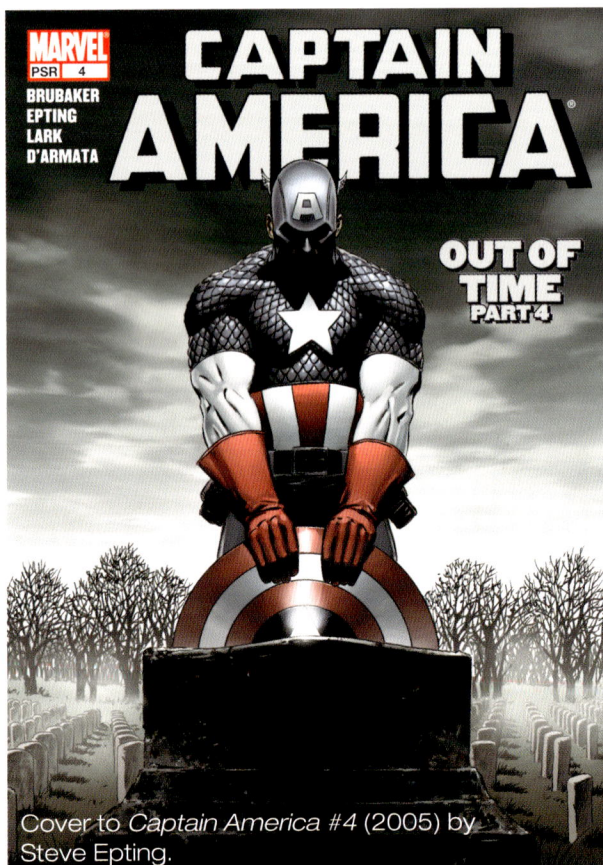

Cover to *Captain America* #4 (2005) by Steve Epting.

Limited-edition print by Paolo Rivera, created as a gift to crew members.

Cover to the Marvel Cinematic Universe tie-in *Captain America: First Vengeance* #1 (2011) by Paolo Rivera.

Captain America: First Vengeance #2 (2011), art from page 1, by Neil Edwards, Danny Miki and Sotocolor.

GIVE HYDRA HELL, CAPTAIN!

Perhaps the most innovative technique used to draw attention to the film was a collaborative venture with Marvel's comic-book division. Continuing the line of official tie-in comics begun with *Iron Man 2: Public Identity* and *Iron Man 2: Agents of S.H.I.E.L.D.* — and premiering on the same night as the vaunted Super Bowl spot — was *Captain America: First Vengeance*, a Marvel Digital Comic debuting on captainamerica.com. Set firmly within the world of the Marvel Cinematic Universe, the eight-issue miniseries was written by Fred Van Lente and illustrated by a host of talented artistic teams: Luke Ross and Richard Isanove; Neil Edwards, Crimelab Studios and Daniel Green, and Sotocolor; Javi Fernandez and Veronica Gandini; and Andy Smith, Tom Palmer and Gandini — with a stunning debut cover artwork by Paolo Rivera. In addition to exploring new corners of Marvel's Cinematic Universe, *First Vengeance* reminds audiences of Captain America's origins as a comic-book character — and heralds his bright future as one of cinema's newest icons.

SOUND OFF FOR EQUIPMENT CHECK!

"RATATATATAT!"

"MRRREEOOOWWW-- BOOOOM!!"

GO GO GO!!

Captain America: First Vengeance #1 (2011), art from pages 1-2, by Luke Ross and Richard Isanove.

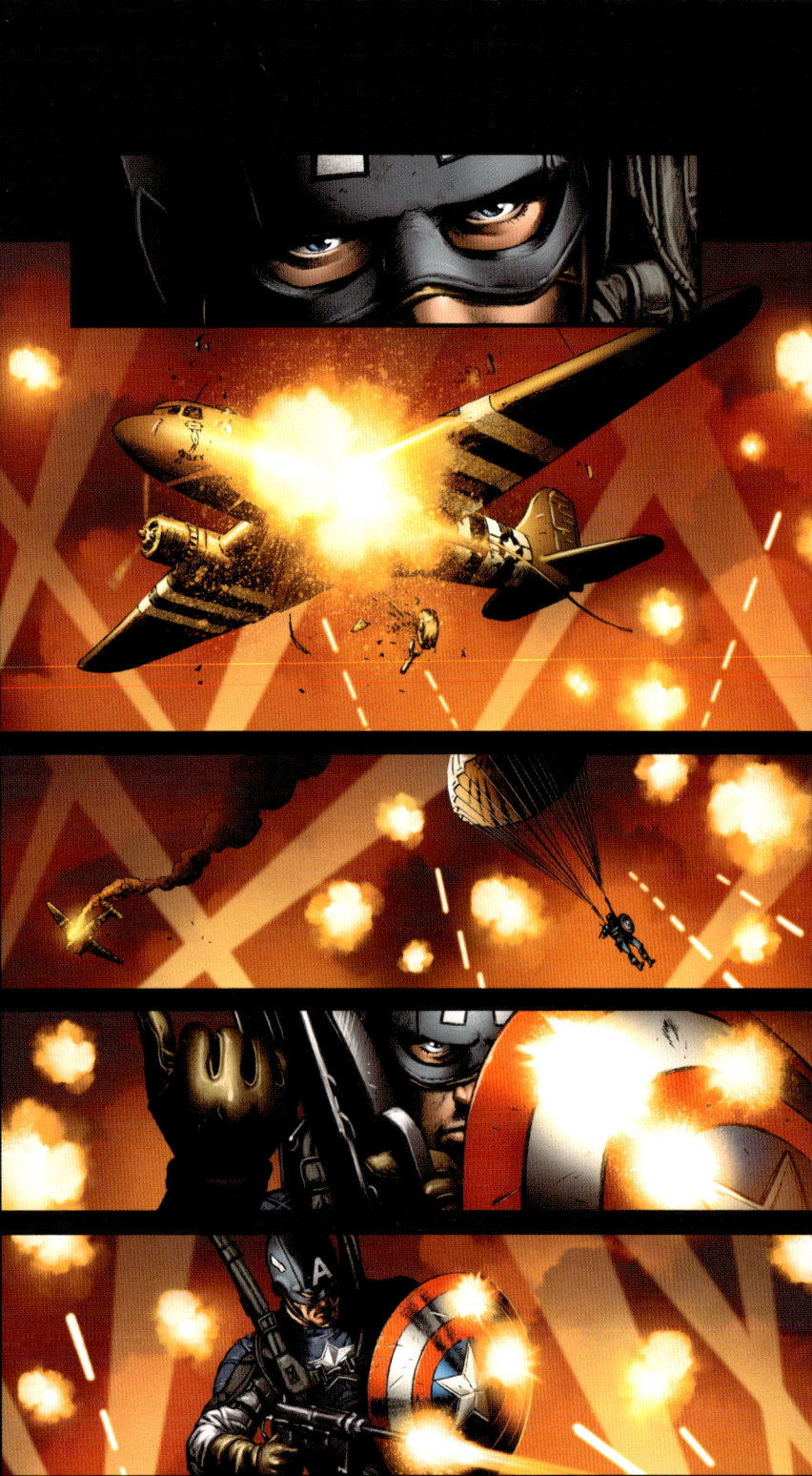

Captain America: First Vengeance #1 (2011), art from pages 5-7,
by Luke Ross and Richard Isanove.

CONTRIBUTOR BIOS 2011

A Hollywood fixture, *Captain America: The First Avenger* Director **Joe Johnston** has had a hand in some of the most memorable adventure films in the genre's history — from his days as art director on *Raiders of the Lost Ark* and the original *Star Wars* trilogy to his work in the director's chair on films including *Honey, I Shrunk the Kids*, *The Rocketeer*, *Jumanji* and *October Sky*. His many achievements include an Academy Award for Best Visual Effects for his work on *Raiders of the Lost Ark*.

Marvel Studios President **Kevin Feige** has guided the studio through more than a decade of films and was instrumental in starting up the current era of movies produced directly by the studio. Feige serves as producer for the studio's entire slate of films — including *Iron Man*, *Iron Man 2*, *The Incredible Hulk*, *Thor*, and the upcoming *Captain America: The First Avenger* and *The Avengers*. In that role, it falls to him to coordinate the emergent Marvel Cinematic Universe between the different productions — drawing together a talented pool of directors, producers, actors and artists to create a coherent film world, the likes of which Hollywood has never attempted.

Louis D'Esposito is co-president of Marvel Studios. He served as executive producer on the blockbuster hits *Iron Man, Iron Man 2, Thor* and *Captain America: The First Avenger*, and is working on Marvel Studios' highly anticipated *The Avengers*. As co-president of the studio and executive producer on all Marvel films, D'Esposito balances running the studio with overseeing each film from development through distribution. D'Esposito began his tenure at Marvel Studios in 2006. D'Esposito's executive-producing credits prior to Marvel include the 2006 hit *The Pursuit of Happyness*, starring Will Smith; *Zathura: A Space Adventure*; and the 2003 hit *S.W.A.T.*, starring Samuel L. Jackson and Colin Farrell.

Victoria Alonso served as co-producer on Director Jon Favreau's *Iron Man* and *Iron Man 2*, Kenneth Branagh's *Thor*, and Joe Johnston's *Captain America: The First Avenger*; she is co-producing Marvel Studios' *The Avengers* for writer/director Joss Whedon. Alonso's career began at the infancy of the visual-effects industry, when she served as a commercial VFX producer. From there, she VFX-produced numerous feature films — working with such directors as Ridley Scott (*Kingdom of Heaven*), Tim Burton (*Big Fish*) and Andrew Adamson (*Shrek*), to name a few. Alonso serves as executive vice president of visual effects and post production for Marvel Studios.

Co-Producer **Stephen Broussard** is Marvel Studios' senior vice president of production and development. Alongside his colleagues in the feature film division, he is responsible for creative oversight of films on the studio's slate. Broussard served as associate producer on Marvel Studios' *The Incredible Hulk*. Since joining Marvel in 2004, Broussard has been involved in films such as *The Fantastic Four, X-Men: The Last Stand* and *Spider-Man 3*. Broussard was part of the team that helped usher in the new era of filmmaking at Marvel Studios whereby Marvel began to independently produce films, of which the first was the blockbuster *Iron Man* in 2008. Broussard attended the Florida State University Graduate Film School, where he produced a short film that went on to win a Student Academy Award.

Costume Designer **Anna B. Sheppard**'s varied film credits include Quentin Tarantino's *Inglorious Basterds*, Peter Webber's *Hannibal Rising*, Michael Mann's *The Insider* and Lee Tamahori's *The Devil's Double*. In 1993, Sheppard earned Academy and BAFTA Award nominations for her work on Steven Spielberg's critically acclaimed masterpiece *Schindler's List*. She has worked on two features with director Roman Polanski: *Oliver Twist* in 2005 and *The Pianist* in 2002 — for which she received her second Academy Award nomination and a César Award nomination, and won Best Costume Design at the Polish Film Awards.

Before **Rick Heinrichs** began work on *Captain America: The First Avenger* as the film's production designer, his résumé already read like an encyclopedia of some of the most visually striking films ever to grace Hollywood. Working in a variety of art-department roles from visual consultant to set designer to art director, Heinrichs had a hand in influential films such as *Beetlejuice*, *Batman Returns*, *Edward Scissorhands*, *Ghostbusters II* and *The Nightmare Before Christmas*. And in his role as production designer, Heinrichs' credits remain just as impressive — including *Fargo*, *The Big Lebowski*, *Hulk*, *Sleepy Hollow*, and the second and third films in the blockbuster *Pirates of the Caribbean* franchise.

Ryan Meinerding has only been a freelance concept artist and illustrator in the film business since 2005, but his work is already drawing the kind of raves reserved for veterans of the industry. After earning a degree in industrial design from Notre Dame, he eventually transitioned to Hollywood and worked on *Outlander*. Subsequent to *Iron Man*, he worked on *Transformers: Revenge of the Fallen* and helped coordinate wardrobe for *Watchmen*. While working on *Iron Man 2*, Meinerding contributed the design for the new Iron Man armor in the comic-book series *Invincible Iron Man*, continuing to cement the strong bonds between Marvel Studios and Marvel Comics. He was part of the *Iron Man* crew nominated for the 2009 Art Directors Guild Excellence in Production Design Award for Fantasy Films, was one of the main concept designers for *Thor*, and served as visual development co-supervisor on *Captain America: The First Avenger* and the upcoming film *The Avengers*.

Charlie Wen has held a variety of positions in the entertainment industry, ranging from concept designer to art director, on everything from feature films to video games and commercials. Wen's client list reads as a virtual who's who of the industry, including Digital Domain, Disney, Dreamworks, Legendary Pictures, Marvel Studios, Darkhorse, Rhythm and Hues, Imagi Studios, Wizards of the Coast, and Sony Computer Entertainment of America. In 2005, he created Kratos and helped establish *God of War* as a monolithic action-adventure title for Sony PlayStation. Outside of the production environment, Charlie has given lectures on figure drawing and character design at many distinguished studios and universities. After helping to establish the main character designs in *Thor*, he holds the title of co-visual development supervisor at Marvel Studios, working on *Captain America: The First Avenger* and the upcoming film *The Avengers*.

David White began his career at age 19 as an assistant to Make-Up Effects Artist Nick Maley in 1982 on *The Keep*, directed by Michael Mann at Shepperton Film Studios. White then went to work for Creature Effects Designer Lyle Conway on *Return to Oz* (1983) as a sculptor, followed by *Lifeforce* (1984). In 1985, White joined the make-up effects team on *Little Shop of Horrors* (1985) as senior painter and animatronics technician of the Audrey II plants. This was the start of a career spanning more than twenty years as both a prosthetic make-up and animatronic designer on many films, TV series and commercials. Following his extensive involvement in Mary Shelley's *Frankenstein* (1994) as a make-up effects designer, White formed his own company, Altered States FX, with business partner Sacha Carter. Based at Shepperton Studios, White went on to work on many different projects, responsible for overseeing all prosthetic work from design concept to final on-set application. The movie *The Hunchback* for TNT saw him receive his first Emmy Award nomination; his prosthetic design work on Robbie Williams in the music video for "Rock DJ" became a multi-award winner for its prosthetic make-up in the Best Special Effects category. He subsequently worked on Ridley Scott's *Kingdom of Heaven* and Tony Scott's *Spy Game*. White has also created prosthetics for films such as *The Da Vinci Code,* and prosthetics for the Oscar-winning make-up on *La Vie en Rose* and off-beat cult classic *In Bruges*. White then turned his attention to heading up FX movies as head of department on films such as Ridley Scott's *Robin Hood* and Joe Johnston's *Captain America: The First Avenger*.

Lead Vehicle Designer **Daniel Simon** graduated in 2000 with honors from the University of Applied Science in Pforzheim, Germany. Between 2000 and 2005, he worked as a car designer for automakers Bugatti, Lamborghini and Volkswagen. In 2005, Simon began freelancing around the world for clients such as Honda, Hermes, Puma and DKNY. His first book — *Cosmic Motors*, published in 2007 — helped him make the transition to Hollywood. As a vehicle designer on Disney's *Tron Legacy* feature film, he helped develop the Light Cycle and many other iconic vehicles. Simon's work has been published in more than 30 countries by magazines such as *GQ*, *Wired*, *Top Gear*, *Playboy* and *Popular Mechanics*.

Visual Effects Supervisor **Christopher Townsend** graduated with a Graphic Design Bachelor of Arts Honors Degree in England in 1988. After six years specializing in graphic design and animation for broadcasting and TV advertising, Townsend began work at George Lucas' esteemed Industrial Light and Magic. During the next eleven years, he worked as an artist and supervisor on some of the most influential visual-effects movies of our time — including the rerelease of the original *Star Wars: A New Hope* and the new trilogy; *Mission: Impossible*; *The Lost World: Jurassic Park*; *AI: Artificial Intelligence*; *Hulk*; and *Pirates of the Caribbean: Dead Man's Chest*. In 2007, he became a freelance visual effects supervisor on *Journey to the Center of the Earth*, and then supervised on location for *X-Men Origins: Wolverine*, oversaw the VFX work for *Ninja Assassin*, supervised on *Percy Jackson and the Lightning Thief* and was the overall VFX supervisor for Marvel's *Captain America: The First Avenger*.

ACKNOWLEDGMENTS

VICTORIA ALONSO

HAYLEY ATWELL

MAURO BORELLI

ADAM BROCKBANK

STEPHEN BROUSSARD

JOHN BUSH

JIM CARSON

PAUL CASTLING

KENNETH CHOI

RODOLFO DAMAGGIO

LEANDER DEENY

LOUIS D'ESPOSITO

JOHN DEXTER

ANITA DHILLON

NEIL EDWARDS

STEVE EPTING

CHRIS EVANS

KEVIN FEIGE

JJ FEILD

BARRY GIBBS

JAMES HEGEDUS

RICK HEINRICHS

RICHARD ISANOVE

JOE JOHNSTON

JACK KIRBY

CHRIS LOWE

JIM MARTIN

STEPHEN MCFEELY

RYAN MEINERDING

DANNY MIKI

ANDY NICHOLSON

ANDY PARK

PAOLO RIVERA

LUKE ROSS

NATHAN SCHROEDER

ANNA B. SHEPPARD

DANIEL SIMON

JOE SIMON

SOTOCOLOR

KAI SPANNUTH

SEBASTIAN STAN

HENRICK TAMM

CHRISTOPHER TOWNSEND

DARRELL WAGNER

HUGO WEAVING

CHARLIE WEN

PADDY WHITAKER

ANDREW WILLIAMSON

ARTIST CREDITS

MAURO BORELLI
PAGES 23, 44-46, 48-59, 92-101, 141, 144, 148-151, 188

ADAM BROCKBANK
PAGE 146

JIM CARSON
PAGES 102-103

PAUL CASTLING
PAGES 136, 156, 164-165, 206-207, 209

RODOLFO DAMAGGIO
PAGES 216-223

JAMES HEGEDUS
PAGES 110, 214-215

RYAN MEINERDING
PAGES 1, 5, 18-22, 26-38, 42, 62-63, 66, 70-79, 82, 85-91, 104-105, 111, 116-117, 122-125, 134-135, 138-140, 152-155, 158-163, 172-173

ANDY PARK
PAGE 196

NATHAN SCHROEDER
PAGES 142-143, 180-181, 188-189

ANNA B. SHEPPARD
PAGES 24, 68-69, 106-107, 108-109, 112-113, 114-115

DANIEL SIMON
PAGES 165, 168-187, 190-195, 197-205, 210-213

HENRICK TAMM
PAGES 126-127, 129-130, 141, 208

CHARLIE WEN
PAGES 40-43, 60-61, 64-65, 72-75, 77, 80-85

DARRELL WAGNER
PAGES 24, 68-69, 106-107, 108-109, 112-113, 114-115

ANDREW WILLIAMSON
PAGE 118

CAPTAIN AMERICA
THE FIRST AVENGER